Overture Publishing
an imprint of

ONEWORLD CLASSICS
London House
243-253 Lower Mortlake Road
Richmond
Surrey TW9 2LL
United Kingdom

This Opera Guide first published by John Calder (Publishers) Ltd in 1982

This new edition of *Falstaff* Opera Guide first published by Overture
Publishing, an imprint of Oneworld Classics Ltd, in 2011

Articles © the authors

© Oneworld Classics Ltd, 2011

English translation of the *Falstaff* libretto © Andrew Porter, 1982

ISBN: 978-0-7145-4414-4

Printed in the United Kingdom

Regina Resnik as Quickly with Geraint Evans at Covent Garden. (photo: Houston Rogers)

Preface

This series, published under the auspices of English National Opera and The Royal Opera, aims to prepare audiences to enjoy and evaluate opera performances. Each book contains the complete text, set out in the original language together with a current performing translation. The accompanying essays have been commissioned as general introductions to aspects of interest in each work. As many illustrations and musical examples as possible have been included because the sound and spectacle of opera are clearly central to any sympathetic appreciation of it. We hope that, as ideal companions to the opera should be, they are well-informed, witty and attractive.

Nicholas John
Series Editor

Falstaff

Giuseppe Verdi

Opera Guides
Series Editor
Nicholas John

OVERTURE

Contents

Illustrations

Introduction

Nicholas John

Even before Shakespeare, whom Verdi so greatly revered, had been exalted by the Romantics as an inspiration to every kind of art, his comedy *The Merry Wives of Windsor* had inspired an opera from Salieri. *Falstaff ossia Le Tre Burle* appeared in 1799; Beethoven composed variations on the aria '*La stessa, la stessissima*'. Falstaff also appeared in Pacini's *La Gioventù di Enrico V* (1820); in Balfe's *Falstaff*, performed in Italian in 1838, and a favourite with the great fat bass Luigi Lablache; in Otto Nicolai's immensely popular *Die Lustigen Weiber von Windsor* (1849), Ambroise Thomas's *Le Songe d'une nuit d'été* (in which Shakespeare and Queen Elizabeth are also characters (1850)) and Adolphe Adam's *Falstaff* (1856). But during the second half of the century, Verdi (at least for foreign opera-goers) 'was' Italian opera and, with the failure of his second opera *Un Giorno di Regno* in 1839, he had turned his back on wholly comic subjects — if not on the occasional comic character or scene. His almost notorious preference for grand tragic themes makes it tempting to see in *Falstaff* the comic reverse of these life-long preoccupations. Its humour is directed against conceit, self-deception and pretentiousness and at the idea that men can be the tyrants of women — the laughing antidote to those vices reviled by Verdi in opera after opera featuring hypocritical, vengeful priests, and women as the innocent victims of insanely jealous husbands, brothers, fathers and lovers.

In 1850 Verdi wrote that 'he had it in mind to set to music *The Tempest* and all the principal plays of the great tragedian'. Thus when he was sent the scenario of *Falstaff* in 1889, he could reply, 'I wanted to reread *The Merry Wives*, both parts of *Henry IV* and *Henry V*' before judging it; '. . . it is excellent'.

His devotion to Shakespeare was shared by his librettist, Arrigo Boito. Boito combined with his musician's training a very distinctive literary flare: his first libretto, written in 1865 when he was 22, was *Hamlet* for his friend Franco Faccio. As a journalist his trenchant criticism of the state of Italian art provoked Verdi to a twenty year antagonism because he mistook it for a personal attack. As a poet and composer his aspirations overshot his abilities: he set both parts of Goethe's *Faust* in his opera *Mefistofele*, but the resulting six hour marathon infuriated the La Scala audience in 1868. A shortened version, however, scored success. His only other opera, *Nerone*, was unfinished, despite a lifetime's work, at his death in 1918.

In the 1870's and 80's Boito was constantly writing for the theatre in a variety of styles. As 'Tobia Gorrio', he wrote *La Gioconda*, a melodrama, for Ponchielli's opera (1876); a comedy in Venetian dialect, *Basi e bote* (eventually set in 1927 by Riccardo Pick-Mangiagalli); and *Iràm* (full of puns and word games) based on *The Arabian Nights*. He translated Wagner's *Rienzi* and *Tristan and Isolde* for the Italian premières; and *Antony and Cleopatra* and *Romeo and Juliet* for his mistress, the actress Eleonora Duse. By the time he came to collaborate with the veteran composer, more than 20 years his senior, on *Otello*, he was Italy's leading literary figure and acutely aware, both as a composer and critic, of how music could tranform the mere words of a libretto.

Verdi's enthusiasm for the project may be guaged from this exchange of letters in July 1889. His objections — of his age, of Boito's composing career — were put; and then he wrote:

A pair of photographs of Verdi and Boito at the time of the première of 'Falstaff' presented to Mrs Stanford, the wife of the musician whose review of the opera is quoted on page 10. (Royal College of Music)

I don't think that writing a comedy should tire you out. A tragedy causes its author *genuinely to suffer*; one's thoughts undergo a suggestion of sadness which renders the nerves morbidly sensitive. The jokes and laughter of comedy exhilarate mind and body. 'A smile adds a thread to life's tapestry.' ...

How are we to overcome these obstacles? Have you a sound argument to oppose to mine? I hope so but I don't believe it ... Still, let's think it over (and take care to do nothing that would harm your career), and if you can find me one, and I can find some way of casting off ten years or so ... then what joy to be able to say to the public: 'Here we are again! Roll up!' ...

Boito's reply includes these remarks:

The fact is that I never think of your age either when I'm talking to you or when I'm writing to you or when I'm working for you ...

When Verdi suffered slight illnesses and became very upset over the news of the insanity and death of Faccio (who had become musical director of La Scala and a favourite conductor), he stopped working. But he started again in the Autumn of 1890 and soon had to confess the truth of certain rumours to his publisher, Giulio Ricordi.

So what's it all about? An opera (quite an undertaking!) in which a 'stripling' makes his debut in comedy — not counting the other comic opera that belongs in the Old Testament! —

And then?... When it is finished?

And then?... Will I ever finish it?

And then? And then?...

I could raise so many 'and then's; but I would prefer to leave them unwritten because they would assume a less comic tone!...

A — — — — — — — — — —men.

Mariano Stabile, considered by many as the greatest Falstaff after Maurel. (Stuart-Liff Collection) He produced the opera at La Fenice and sang the role in 1959 when he was 70. Richard Bonynge reported a 'wonderfully youthful sound, resonant and with the required staying-power for this mammoth part and a line to be envied and copied by most singers half his age'. (Opera)

Once he admitted the possibility of a public performance at La Scala, he began casting it. Julian Budden points out (*The Operas of Verdi, Vol. 3*) that it was to be 'above all an opera of teamwork'; and Victor Maurel (the baritone who had created Iago) almost lost the title role through his exorbitant demands to have the sole right to sing it. The exuberance of Verdi's correspondence communicates the high spirits in which the opera was written. By 1891, the vocal score was done; the orchestration was complete the following year. 'Certain passages', Verdi told a reporter in 1893, 'are so droll that the music has often made me laugh while writing it.'

After the triumphant first performance Verdi angrily realised that he would have to make a couple of alterations to secure the effects he wanted:

> It would have been so easy to do! What wretched heads we have! Better to dash them against a wall!

But even before these improvements had been made, the world had already registered its approval. C.V. Stanford reporting for the London Graphic, concluded with a description that has stood the test of time; the opera was:

> Clear as crystal in construction, tender and explosive by turns, humorous and witty without a touch of extravagance or a note of vulgarity.

'A Lyric Comedy Unlike Any Other'

Michael Rose

'Tonight, then *Falstaff*... I don't know whether I have found the gay note, the true note, above all the sincere note. Alas, there are many beautiful things in the music of today — and sometimes real progress (provided they don't go too far) — but in general there's no sincerity, and everybody wants to be like everybody else...'

Thus Verdi to Camille Bellaigue on the day of the first performance of *Falstaff*. As always, what concerned him was the substance of what he had written, not the form in which it was expressed. Yet for others, seeing *Falstaff* for the first time, it was perhaps inevitable that it should be the novelty of the forms which made the first impression. Only a few days earlier his wife, Giuseppina, had written to her sister:

'Last night I went for the first time to rehearsal, and if I must judge with my head and my heart, it seems to me the beginning of a new *genre*, even the appearance of a new art, music and poetry! But we will see how it is received by the Great Arbiter, the Respected Public!'

The public, of course, received *Falstaff* with enthusiasm. It could hardly have done otherwise, with Verdi only a few months from his eightieth birthday, the Grandest of Grand Old Men with a lifetime of profoundly popular operatic success behind him. The musical world was present in Milan to do him homage, and after the performance the Milanese crowds thronged his hotel and forced him to appear several times on the balcony. Even the Scala orchestra was only prevented at the last moment from serenading him in the street below....

Yet *Falstaff* never became a popular success. Verdi himself hadn't thought it would: when Giulio Ricordi wrote in trepidation, asking the composer to name his own figure for the publication rights of the opera, Verdi asked no more than he had asked for *Otello* six years before. 'No, no, my dear Giulio, no thanks. I know what I have done. *Falstaff* is not, nor ever will be, a commercial opera. I have written it, not for you, nor for the public, but for my own satisfaction. It is only just that you should not be ruined over what I have done for my personal enjoyment.'

Again and again, during the composition of *Falstaff*, comes this idea of personal enjoyment. 'I started to write *Falstaff* simply to pass the time', he wrote to Ricordi in 1891, 'without preconceived ideas, without plans — I repeat, simply to pass the time! Nothing else!' And five months later: 'It is too soon yet to talk about *Falstaff*, which is going very slowly. And anyhow, I am becoming more and more convinced that the vastness of La Scala will spoil its effect. In writing *Falstaff* I haven't given a thought either to theatres or to singers; I have written for my own pleasure, just for myself, and I really believe that instead of La Scala it ought to be given at Sant' Agata' (that is at his home). 'Will he finish it, or won't he?' wrote Giuseppina, 'Will he ever produce it? Only time can tell, no one else, not even he himself. The object was to keep him occupied and happy, and this it is doing...'

Now all this is very strange for Verdi, who throughout his life had seen himself, if not as a servant of the public, at least as very much dependent on it for his artistic justification. His operas, from the earliest days right up to the triumphs of *Aida* and *Otello*, had been firmly entrenched in a concept of the theatre which took the audience as its central, unchanging fact, and had been composed always as logical

Lawrence Tibbett as Ford, the role in which he triumphed at the Met. in 1925. He subsequently sang the title role. (Ida Cook Collection)

developments of a tradition in which that audience felt at home. Yet here he is, for the first time, in a totally different frame of mind, literally playing around with musical ideas for their own sake. 'You are working, I hope?' he wrote to Boito while waiting for the libretto of the first Act; 'the curious thing is that I am working too! I am amusing myself by writing fugues! Yes, sir, fugues, and a comic fugue that might come in well in *Falstaff*. But what is a comic fugue — why comic? you will say. I don't know what or why, but it *is* a comic fugue.'

It is small wonder, then, that the first audiences did not take to this opera as immediately as they had done to its predecessors. There is a fleeting quality about it; the melodic invention is more prodigal than ever, but unrepetitive; tunes come and go almost before they can be grasped. This, for us, is one of its greatest charms, but for the original audiences it was puzzling. They found, too, that after the excitement of the linen-basket scene at the end of Act Two, the third Act represented a falling off, and they were not at once convinced by the contrasting atmosphere of fantasy with which Boito (who had sensed this danger all along) so subtly invested these final scenes, nor by the amazingly delicate beauty of the music which Verdi wove around it. And then there was the final fugue, which concluded the opera as no comic opera had ever been concluded before, of a length and contrapuntal complexity that were musically disconcerting: not particularly beautiful to the nineteenth-century Italian ear, and certainly not to be expected in the framework of a nineteenth-century Italian *opera buffa*.

Falstaff has often been quoted as the last great flower of the Italian *buffa* tradition, and there is indeed a sense in which it can be so regarded. But if the great Italian tradition may have provided the general background against which the septuagenarian composer fitted together the sparkling thematic mosaic of his score, the final result far outstripped, both in form and in substance, any concrete model that he could possibly have had in mind.

The origins of Italian *opera buffa*, as a form of its own, go back to the first years of the eighteenth century, and in particular to Naples. The disordered jumble into which the operatic libretto had fallen by the end of the seventeenth century brought an inevitable reaction in the reforms of Apostolo Zeno and later Metastasio, whose austere and high-minded style excluded humour entirely from the libretto of the eighteenth-century *opera seria*, and it was no doubt mainly in reaction to this development that a taste for independent comic opera began to grow. As a result, *opera buffa* automatically became everything that the severe and stylized *opera seria* was not, and this in turn imposed upon it from the start certain conventions and limitations of its own. By the middle of the century the new form had established itself all over Italy as the accepted alternative to *opera seria*; as a contrast its natural expressiveness and vivacity, entirely free from lofty gestures and vocal exhibitionism, came to be increasingly appreciated not only by the audiences at which it had originally been aimed, but also by the more intelligent opera-goers. Piccinni, Paisiello and Cimarosa were the great names of *opera buffa* in the later eighteenth century, and each made contributions to the form which left their mark — Piccinni in the development of ensembles and finales, Paisiello in the warmth of feeling and expression he infused into the form, Cimarosa in the crisp brilliance and elegance of his comic style.

All these characteristics were of course taken up, developed and ultimately transcended by the greatest of all composers of *opera buffa*, Mozart. But Mozart was not an Italian, his musical world was fundamentally different, and he formed no part of the Italian tradition from which Verdi so patently sprang. The composer who continued the purely Italian line of *opera buffa* into the nineteenth century was Rossini, and he did so with an ebullience, wit and utterly anti-romantic charm that represent an opposite pole from Mozart, even if in sheer technical brilliance he is one of the very few composers who can bear comparison with him.

For most people, Rossini is the culmination of *opera buffa*, the *Barber* its final and most characteristic product. But Rossini is really something of a sport in musical history, the projection of a classical ideal into a romantic age: while we may admit the wistful appeal of a figure like *La Cenerentola* there is in general little of humanity in his most typical characters, only a perfection of artifice and musical style, parody, urbanity, humour and charm. He carries on the most eighteenth-century aspect of *opera buffa*, now even more sharply pointed by comparison with the new world around it, and he gives away very, very little of himself. Donizetti on the other hand stands nearer to the dividing line: his comic operas are the only ones after Rossini that deserve mention in the same breath as his, but here there is a tenderness mixed with the humour that recalls the expressive warmth of Paisiello, and the list of his operas includes a significant number classified as *semiseria* — in itself an indication of a swing away from the purely *buffa* tradition. And indeed, after Donizetti, the old *buffa* tradition is clearly on its way out. There is an occasional good piece, and quite often a successful one, but the Ricci brothers, Petrella, Pedrotti, Cagnoni, are not names that mean a great deal today, and the works they produced are by and large the last variations of a form that was essentially of the eighteenth century, and of which Rossini was unquestionably the last real master.

To this company, in fact, belongs Verdi's only previous attempt at a comic subject, *Un Giorno di Regno*. His second opera, written at the age of twenty-six during the period immediately following the death of his young wife, it was a disastrous failure and was hissed off the stage of La Scala after only one performance. As a matter of fact, its reception was hardly justified by the quality of the music, which is attractive in a fairly unremarkable post-Rossinian vein, and as Verdi himself said many years later 'who knows how many others, no better, have been tolerated and even applauded. . . .'. But Romani's libretto was an unfortunate choice for someone of Verdi's temperament (in fact, he didn't choose it: it was one of a handful of comedies provided by the management of La Scala, from which he picked out 'the one that seemed the least bad'): it is entirely and irrevocably in the classic *opera buffa* mould, quite without the sentiment and delicacy of the same librettist's *Elisir d'Amore* of eight years before, and unlike Donizetti the young Verdi was unable to drag the Rossinian style into the Romantic age. He was in any case the last person who should have tried to do so: the whole history of his development over the next fifty years shows that two of his strongest characteristics as a composer were his rich human involvement with his characters, and his impatience with the forms of received operatic practice. Faced with a libretto so uncompromisingly *buffo*, he lacked entirely the deft touch of the experienced practitioner which might have got it past the Scala audience, nor did he possess the peculiar transforming gift which enabled Donizetti, two years later, to produce a masterpiece in *Don Pasquale*.

Whether Verdi, like some of his more perceptive critics, felt that *Un Giorno di Regno* marked a step in the wrong direction, or whether the traumatic circumstances of its composition and reception created some sort of mental block where comic opera was concerned, the fact is that from that date on he devoted himself exclusively to tragedy on the operatic stage. There are occasional touches of humour in these works: Bernard Shaw, writing about *Falstaff* in 1893, pointed to the conspirators in *Ballo in Maschera*, to the Quintet in the second scene of the same opera, and to Cassio's drinking song in the first Act of *Otello*. 'The grim humour of Sparafucile, the terrible ironic humour of Iago, the agonized humour of Rigoletto: these surely settled the question as to Verdi's capacity for Falstaff none the less because the works in which they occur are tragedies and not comedies. All that could be said on the other side was that Verdi was no Mozart, which was as idle as saying that Victor Hugo was no Molière. Verdi's vein of humour is all the more Shakespearean on that account.'

Which is of course precisely the point, and precisely the reason why the typical *opera buffa* libretto was no use to him. Yet in 1879, when Ricordi had incautiously allowed a reference in his house magazine to Rossini's old dictum that Verdi would never write a comedy, Verdi's reaction was immediate: 'For twenty years I have been searching for a libretto for a comic opera, and now you, with this article of yours, have put it into the public's head to hiss my opera off the stage before it is even written. . . '. Memories of *Un Giorno di Regno*? Possibly — and another letter, written in the same month, betrays a similar concern: ' . . . an opera, or a psalm, or a mass or quartet or symphony, or perhaps an opera buffa! . . . A comic opera, yes, that would be great fun. . . at least, before the staging began'. But it was Giuseppina who put her finger on what was really needed: 'If some librettist were to find a really charming subject which, without being grossly farcical, was genuinely comic, pungent and seductive; a subject with a thread of sentiment woven into it, but woven only so as to temper delicately and pleasantly the bursting gaiety of the laughter — if only a librettist could discover some such subject Verdi, I swear to you, would show himself in an altogether new light'.

Now if *Otello* proved one thing more than Verdi's continuing vitality as a composer, it was Boito's ability, and sensibility, as a librettist. His adaptation of *Othello* had been masterly beyond praise, his goodwill towards Verdi beyond question. But there at least he had been working in a form in which Verdi was already at home: for all its powerful originality, *Otello* is a development of what had gone before. What was needed now was something entirely different, entirely new. 'What can I tell you?' wrote Verdi to Gino Monaldi at the end of 1890: 'For the past forty years I've been wondering about a comic opera, and for the past fifty I've known *The Merry Wives of Windsor*. Alas, the usual ubiquitous "buts" have always got in the way. Now Boito has swept them aside and provided me with a lyric comedy utterly unlike any other. . . '.

Just what it is that makes Boito's text so different is not easy to define precisely, though it is evident on every page of the opera. Certainly, *Falstaff* has little to do with stock *opera buffa*, either in its construction, its characters or its language, and indeed in some ways it is even further from that world than the original play itself. Traditionally it is said that *The Merry Wives* was written, in a rather uninspired hurry, to satisfy a request by Queen Elizabeth to see Falstaff in love; the result is a comparatively conventional farce, episodic in construction and with its hero sadly diluted, that cannot be counted among Shakespeare's greatest works. But Boito, having cut and pruned the action, eliminated characters, and reduced Shakespeare's twenty-five scenes to six, then set about rebuilding the character of Falstaff as he appears in the chronicle plays, lifting ideas wholesale from both parts of *Henry IV* to round out the figure of the fat knight and restore to him something of the paradoxical nobility which he had possessed in the historical plays but largely lost in his creator's dutiful obedience to a royal command. The poetic language of the new version, as well as the variety and flexibility of the rhythmic structure, certainly have nothing of the conventional about them, and if the former is of a quality only to be expected from a professional writer of Boito's distinction, the latter derives at least as much from his own experience as an operatic composer. Indeed, there is something almost

Scotti as Falstaff at the Met. in 1925.

uncanny about the way in which Boito seems to anticipate Verdi's needs, and one feels that there is perhaps a very special truth in the words he wrote to the composer after completing the libretto of *Otello*: 'If I have been able to divine the potent musical qualities of Shakespeare's tragedy and express them in my libretto, it is because I have seen them in terms of Verdi's art, because in writing these verses I have felt what you would feel in illustrating them with that other language, a thousand times more intimate and powerful, the language of music'. Surely no other librettist ever established so mutually sensitive and understanding a relationship with the composer he wrote for.

The vigour and assurance with which Verdi plunged into the opera are ample proof of his feelings about Boito's libretto. The first scene of *Falstaff* goes at a breathtaking pace (very breathtaking if Verdi's own timing of 14 minutes is to be taken as accurate), and incidentally provides the singer of the title role with one of the most exhausting opening scenes in the operatic repertory. Indeed, it is curious to see how Verdi, on first coming to grips with his Shakespearean protagonist, endows him in this first scene with an almost heroic dimension: Falstaff here seems even larger than life, and also larger than anywhere else in the opera. But there is no harm in this, and the vivid intensity of this first impression establishes a capital reserve in terms of characterisation which enriches the whole of the rest of the action.

For Falstaff is not just the central figure of the opera, he is its whole and only *raison d'être*. Around him the passions and human emotions of the other characters wash like waves beating on a rock: the anger of Doctor Caius, the indignation of Mistress Quickly, the love of Nannetta and Fenton, the jealous fury of Ford, the unforced gaiety of the Merry Wives, all these are the stuff from which the music is made, and all are woven together around the central figure of the fat knight. He himself remains in some ways an enigma, as he must, but the conclusion of the opera makes it clear what Verdi felt about him, and looking back we can see that, although he is all humour, all comedy, yet throughout there has always been something of affection, something of understanding, that prevents him from ever becoming unsympathetic.

A substance so subtle, so very much more mature in its intentions than that of the the normal *opera buffa*, inevitably demanded new forms for its expression. The miracle is not only that Boito found them but that Verdi was able to strike the true note, above all the sincere note in setting them. Bernard Shaw, applauding the 'fulness of insight and perfect mastery of workmanship in *Falstaff*', explains the miracle:

> Verdi has exchanged the excess of his qualities for the wisdom to supply his deficiencies; his weaknesses have disappeared with his superfluous force; and he is now, in his dignified competence, the greatest of living dramatic composers. It is not often that a man's strength is so immense that he can remain an athlete after bartering half of it to old age for experience; but the thing happens occasionally, and need not so greatly surprise us in Verdi's case, especially those of us who, long ago, when Von Bulow and others were contemptuously repudiating him, were able to discern in him a man possessing more power than he knew how to use, or indeed was permitted to use by the old operatic forms imposed on him by circumstances . . . '

In *Falstaff* the Verdi method reaches its ultimate degree of refinement. There is a quality in this score that is unlike any other in the history of opera. Echoes of it occur in the works of Verdi's successors: in *Gianni Schicchi*, for example, and in the first act of *La Bohème* (Puccini had been at the first performance of *Falstaff*, and was working on his own opera later in the same year). But the symphonic style of Puccini and his contemporaries was poles apart from this latest Verdian manner, and Verdi had been suspicious of it from the start. 'I have heard the composer Puccini well spoken of', he wrote in 1884; 'he follows the modern tendency, which is natural ... but it seems that in his music the symphonic element predominates. Nothing wrong in this — only, it is necessary to go carefully. Symphony is symphony, and I do not believe it is good, in an opera, to include symphonic passages just for the fun of making the orchestra dance ...'

No, it is not forward, towards the symphonism of Puccini, that *Falstaff* looks, nor backward to any nostalgic memory of the eighteenth century. Here the balance between the human protagonist and his musical accompaniment reaches an equilibrium rarely heard in opera, and the orchestral manner of *Otello* is finally transmuted into something nearer to chamber music, recalling rather the quartets of Beethoven in the intimacy of its expressive style and the easy skill of its contrapuntal interplay. 'Good operas have always been rare, in all periods', wrote Verdi, 'now they are almost non-existent. Why? you will ask. Because we make too much music; because we search too hard; because by peering into the obscurity we lose touch with the sun ...' *Falstaff* is not an old opera nor a new opera, it is simply a unique opera, a lyric comedy unlike any other ...

'Full of Nimble, Fiery and Delectable Shapes'

(Henry IV, Part Two)

David Cairns

When Boito told the still hesitant Verdi that there was only one way he could end his career better than with *Otello* and that was with *Falstaff*, he showed a much greater knowledge of his man than did those critics who could not get over the fact that Verdi of all people should have written a comic opera. Boito himself predicted the surprise that *Falstaff* would cause. 'After expressing all the griefs and lamentations of the human heart, to finish with a mighty burst of laughter — that will astonish the world!' Rossini had declared that Verdi was incapable of treating a comic subject. Yet, as Boito understood, the old man had it abundantly in him to do so. The creator of Fra Melitone in *La forza del destino* did not have to prove his capacity for comedy. There were not, perhaps, many anticipations in his earlier works of the fleet-footed, effervescent music demanded by such a subject as *The Merry Wives of Windsor*, but what there were — in *Rigoletto*, in *Un ballo in maschera* —were sufficient. In *Otello* itself there is music that could go straight into *Falstaff* without incongruity — that is waiting to do so, we can say with hindsight. In order to compose the work, Verdi had no need to become somebody different from what he had been, and in composing it he did not abandon his existing manner. The only essential alteration is in the setting; the style, though further developed and strengthened by that process of constant refinement to which Verdi patiently subjected himself, remains what it was. All that he needed was the spur of a good libretto.

Verdi, in fact, had been looking for one for many years. Boito provided him with it. The libretto of *Falstaff* is a masterpiece of construction and of characterisation. Impossible to imagine the adaptation of a comedy to the operatic stage better done. It is a study in itself to observe how Boito tightened and clarified the action, reducing the number of scenes and characters but borrowing many telling details from those that were cut, in order to enrich those that remained. Thus the text of Ford's soliloquy in the Garter Inn is formed by conflating two different passages (*Merry Wives* II 2 and III 5) in such a way as to intensify the expression of jealous rage and create the vehicle for a great Verdi baritone monologue. The idea for the marvellously comic conclusion to the same scene — Falstaff and Ford at the door of the inn, each outdoing the other in *politesse* — is derived from an exchange between Anne Page and Slender — 'Come on, sir. — Mistress Anne. . . yourself shall go first. — Not I, sir! pray you keep on', etc. — but given a quite different emphasis.* Such examples could be multiplied many times.

Boito's skill, however, is far from being confined to turning a sprawling play into a well-made libretto. In adapting the play he transformed it. *The Merry Wives of Windsor* made liberal use of an earlier, non-Shakespearean text, and achieved much of its undoubted comic verve at the cost of debasing the great creation of the History Plays into a stock figure of fun. Boito, by a brilliant piece of literary

---

* Slender does not figure in the opera — his role as victim of Bardolph's thievery in the opening scene is transferred to Dr Caius — and Anne Page (whose father, an important character in *The Merry Wives*, is also suppressed) is metamorphosed into Nannetta Ford. Among other things, these changes make possible Falstaff's superb '*Caro buon Messer Ford . . . lo scornato, chi è?* in the final scene.

surgery, restored the original, the true Falstaff. The libretto is strengthened, again and again, by graftings from the two parts of *Henry IV*. From Part One come the 'Honour' speech, the evocation of Bardolph's glowing nose lighting the way from tavern to tavern, the reading of the landlord's bill; from Part Two the disquisition on the merits of sack, the 'whole school of tongues in this belly of mine... not a tongue of which speaks any other word but my name', and the proud sally 'I am not only witty in myself but the cause that wit is in other men', which in the opera becomes Falstaff's crowning riposte to the lesser spirits who tried to put him down.

Nor is it just a matter of a few famous set-pieces interpolated into the action of *The Merry Wives*. The entire libretto is alive with the language of the *Henry IV* plays; and these additions have been woven deftly and seamlessly into the fabric of the comedy. The Honour speech from the Battle of Shrewsbury (*Henry IV Part One*) comes in pat on cue to fill out the hint provided in *The Merry Wives* ('You'll not bear a letter from me, you rogue! You stand upon your honour!' etc.): the whole monologue is a masterly conjunction of two separate Shakespearean sources. Falstaff's expostulation after his ducking (*Merry Wives* III 5) is spiced and deepened by phrases from the very similar opening of the great scene which follows Falstaff's return from the Gadshill expedition in *Henry IV Part One* : 'Is there no virtue extant... if manhood, good manhood be not forgot upon the face of earth... a bad world, I say'.

By replacing the fat butt of the *Merry Wives* with the philosopher-knave of *Henry IV*, Boito gave Verdi the opportunity to create an authentically Shakespearean work such as a comic opera based on *The Merry Wives* alone could not have been. He gave him the opportunity, too, for a great reassertion of life after the vision of hatred and self-destruction unloosed in *Otello*. It is as if Verdi needed *Falstaff*, not only to round off his achievement and complete his *œuvre*, but to free himself, to breathe deeply again and purge his system of poison secreted during the composition of *Otello*. This is not merely fanciful. At times the score of *Falstaff* performs what amounts to an act of exorcism, cleansing the musical images, ridding them of their evil spirits. The harsh unisons of Iago's hideous *Credo* become a thing of warmth, of 'laughter holding both its sides', in Mistress Quickly's salutation to Falstaff in the Garter Inn, '*Reverenza*'; the Willow Song's aching sighs are transmuted into Nannetta's radiant call to the nymphs and elfs of Windsor Forest; and the *Credo*'s writhing trills turn to delight as Jack Falstaff celebrates the life-quickening power of the grape. *Falstaff* is more than a brilliantly amusing opera. It is, in Boito's words, a source of 'intellectual joy'; it is a vindication of the world and of humanity's incorrigible optimism in the face of every possible discouragement.

The refining of Verdi's powers that it represents, even by comparison with *Otello*, should not mislead us into assuming that those powers are on the wane. Shaw was wrong when he described *Falstaff* as 'lighted and warmed by the afterglow of the fierce noonday heat of *Ernani*'. 'The gain in beauty', he added, 'conceals the loss in heat.' But there is no loss in heat — on the contrary. *Falstaff* is a work of solar strength; the heat is merely more concentrated. The stimulus of the subject released in Verdi, in his late 70's, an energy hitherto untapped even by him. What was concealed, from those early listeners, was the prodigious force of invention that drives the score. It was concealed by characteristics that people did not generally asssociate with Verdi: humour, lightness of touch, brevity, cleverness and delicacy of workmanship, harmonic sophistication, subtle motivic cross-referencing, long-spanned musical continuity and the almost complete abandonment of the formally distinct 'number' which can be extracted and performed separately. But such qualities need not be a substitute for power, and they are not in *Falstaff*. The absence of numbers is not loss but gain in a score as melodically generous as this. The whole thing is melody. Once you get used to the speed at which things happen, once you know it well enough to be able to catch its beauties on the wing, you realise that you are in possession of one of the richest and most rejuvenating works in all music.

Act One

Part One: *the interior of the Garter Inn*
A crashing C major chord on the offbeat, followed by a swaggering downward flourish and a rising 'oompah' figure of the utmost self-assurance [1], shows us Sir John Falstaff at ease in his armchair, preparing to make his fortune: he is holding sealing-wax to a candle-flame and sealing two letters. The music turns to, an angry E minor as Dr Caius bursts in, shouting that the knight has broken into his property and maltreated his servants. Falstaff at first takes no notice, and calls imperiously for sack. Then, to an expansive figure in E major rising majestically through four octaves and decorated by impudent woodwind figures [2], he blandly admits to the charge, but proposes to do nothing about it. The enraged doctor is no more successful with Bardolph, who — he claims — got him drunk the day before and picked his pockets. Bardolph, in reply (a skittish little triplet on flute and piccolo) merely shows him his flaming nose and asks for a prescription for his ruined insides. Dr Caius turns to Pistol: it must have been him. The offended Ancient snatches up a broom and threatens the doctor, and a violent exchange of insults ensues, to the noisy accompaniment of [1], now recurring every two bars of rapid tempo instead of every three, as at the beginning. Falstaff imposes order; then, to [2] in the home key of C, sits in judgment on the case. Bardolph rejects the accusation: Dr Caius fell asleep under the table, dead drunk, and dreamed his money was stolen. Well, do you hear? asks Falstaff suavely; the matter is decided, the case is dismissed. The fuming, tight-lipped Caius beats a retreat, swearing (emphatic trombone chords) that if he ever goes drinking again it will be with sober, law-abiding, pious men. He makes a brave but rather pathetic show of his exit line, and is ushered unceremoniously from the room, to a final reappearance of [1] in the orchestra. Bardolph and Pistol cap his parting speech with a crude parody 'Amen'.

At last the pace of this quick-fire scene (constructed in masterly fashion out of a combination of [1] and [2]) can slacken. But Falstaff is in no mood for horseplay. Silencing his followers, who are but clumsy artists in crime, he draws the moral, the music sliding with ironic courtesy into A flat major: 'when they steal, let them steal with grace and in the right time.' Then, to an impatient version of the skittish triplet, he turns to more serious matters: the landlord's bill, which he reads out above a bare, expectant open fifth on the horns (which changes charmingly to a glinting chord on flute and piccolo for 'one anchovy'). While he goes on reading out the items he commands Bardolph to look in his purse. But all it contains is two marks and a penny. So that is what he has been brought to! The drunken sot will be his ruin! His lantern of a nose may have lit them without torches through the night on their rounds from one tavern to the next — and the music, with an echo of the rhythm of the downward flourish in [1], settles into an ambling F major [3], rising in a grand curve of phrase as Falstaff acknowledges the pre-eminence of Bardolph's fiery protuberance — but the cost of the wine that has gone to fuel that fire more than outweighs such economies. Pistol is just as extravagant. Falstaff has now worked himself up into a towering indignation.

Pausing only to thunder for sack (the rhythmic figure, still prominent, braying out on all three trumpets), he pictures the two of them wasting his substance, and contemplates the ghastly contradiction of a thin Falstaff (a cavernous, wizened *pianissimo* on piccolo and cello). No one would love him any more. But how could that possibly be? For in this mighty belly of his are a thousand tongues, all speaking his name. At this, the orchestra modulates into a ripe D flat major and an imposing theme rolls out on horns, trumpets and lower woodwind [4], while Bardolph and Pistol acclaim *'Falstaff immenso'* in tones of solemn admiration. Yes, it is his kingdom; and he must enlarge it. But how? Falstaff unfolds his plan. There is a rich merchant in Windsor called Ford whose wife holds the purse-strings. Alice is her name, she is beautiful, and she favours old Jack Falstaff. The music, which began lightly and with an air of studied casualness, broadens out into an ardent tenderness as Falstaff, carried away by his nimble fancy, rehearses her charms. To the swaggering rhythm of [4] he recalls how his heart flamed up one day in response to her smile. Her glance travelled with answering fire across his goodly frame and said as plainly as words, 'I'm yours, Sir John Falstaff'. There is another too, Meg Page; she too is hot for him. The two of them will be his treasure-trove, his Gold Coast. Why not? He is in the Indian summer of his age; and, with a delicious modulation to B major, the rising-and-falling four-note figure which has been made to yield such a wealth of amorous yearning throughout this section returns once more at *'San Martino'* (Indian summer), with an innocence which there is no resisting. Pistol and Bardolph resist, however. To Falstaff's astonishment and indignation, they refuse to deliver the two letters he has written, one to Mistress Ford, the other to Mistress Page. Pistol, with portentous dignity, declines to play the Pandar; Bardolph loftily explains that his honour will not allow him. While the page-boy scampers off with the letters, Falstaff turns wrathfully on his cringing followers. Honour! Them? Sewers of iniquity! The monumental scorn he heaps on them is expressed in music of wonderful vividness and pungency. Note the way, after 'Your honour! What's honour? I'll tell you!', the orchestra seems to shake the two rogues like a dog shaking a rat, so angry are its trills. Much of this great scene is in a kind of recitative, with the voice unaccompanied. (An exception is the confession that 'even he' has had on occasion to 'leave the fear of God on the left hand, and hide mine honour in my necessity', set to music of disarmingly churchy blandness — see musical example (a).) But the superbly resourceful scoring of the orchestral interjections mirrors every flight of Falstaff's fancy and every fine shade of his scorn and sarcasm; and gradually the triplet motif of his 'Can honour feed a man when he's hungry?' etc. takes charge of the monologue and becomes the agent of the musical development. It has almost the last word, blaring out derisively on solo trumpet and woodwind, as Falstaff, his patience exhausted, seizes the broom and sweeps Bardolph and Pistol summarily from his sight.

Part Two: *a garden; Ford's house on the left, groups of trees in the centre.*
The quicksilver brilliance of the merry wives' music is immediately established by the rapid, smiling patter and darting harmonic asides of the opening 16-bar passage in E major for staccato woodwind and horns [5]. Their musical idiom is light, pointed, always on the move, and gives a constant sense both of neat deportment and of just-suppressed laughter; but it is also intensely lyrical. Despite the conversational form and the brief and animated exchanges between the characters, the musical action is conducted melodically; the whole scene sings, and the listener is carried along as by a single melodic impulse. This is

The ladies of Windsor in Zeffirelli's 1961 Covent Garden production; left to right: Mirella Freni, Mariella Angioletti, Regina Resnik, Josephine Veasey. (photo: Anthony Crickmay)

characteristic of the merry wives' music throughout the opera.

Falstaff's letters have been delivered, and as the curtain rises we see Meg Page, accompanied by Mistress Quickly, hurrying with her letter to Alice Ford to tell her all about it, just as the unsuspecting Alice, with her daughter Nannetta, comes out of the house carrying hers, en route for Page's house. To their further astonishment, the letters are identical save for the names. They read them aloud, to a humorous but shapely melody on the cor anglais, the bottom note of which is supplied with droll effect by the clarinet (a fine example of instrumental limitations being turned to creative use) [6]. As the tone of Falstaff's love-offering grows more impassioned, the courtly phrases broaden into more and more expansive melody, culminating in the richly parodistic *'e il viso tuo'* ('your radiant glances') [7], sung by Alice with deliberate extravagance (and ending with the comic emphasis on the supertonic which is such a feature of the opera). It provokes a gurgle of laughter from all four women. Then, remembering that they are respectable people, they wax indignant and plot a grisly revenge on the fat knight for his scandalous presumption [8].

As they move away and are lost to sight among the trees, Ford, Dr Caius, Fenton, Bardolph and Pistol enter from the right, deep in whispered conversation. Their agitated 2/4 [9] soon mingles with the 6/8 of the women [8], still hidden from view in the trees. When the hubbub of their composite ensemble dies down, it emerges that Pistol is telling the horrified Ford about Falstaff's designs on his wife, and about the letter Falstaff has sent, which — he and Bardolph sanctimoniously add — they refused to deliver. Ford must be on his guard, or he will soon find himself wearing a pair of horns. At this point the two groups spot each other (though each remains independent of the other, and neither group has any notion that they are both plotting against Falstaff). There is a general exit to either side of the stage, but not before Alice has remarked that Ford is of a jealous temperament. Nannetta and Fenton are left alone, and we have the first of those brief, fugitive love scenes which Verdi, in Boito's phrase, 'sprinkled' over the opera — music of a sweet, heart-piercing freshness which is not the least miraculous achievement of a composer nearing his 80s [10]. As always, the young lovers' hurried conversation is cut short; they separate, calling to one another, their magical phrases [11] accompanied at first by a single high oboe, then by [10] stealing in again with exquisite effect on *pianissimo* strings.

The next moment the merry wives and Mistress Quickly reappear, to a busy unison motif derived from the rhythmic introduction to [3] (itself, of course, a derivation of [1]). They are still scheming against Falstaff, and Nannetta rejoins them. To a slower, playful theme on the violins, Alice instructs Mistress Quickly to go to the Garter and offer Falstaff an assignation with her. Then the quicker tempo returns, with much contrapuntal activity in the strings, and the downfall of the fat knight is further discussed. The music rises to a climax, then breaks off as they disperse at the sight of a male figure among the trees. It is Fenton; he and Nannetta briefly resume their mock warfare, this time to a more active and spirited accompaniment. Again they are interrupted, and their love-play dissolves once more into the enchantment of [11].

Now it is the men who re-enter, to an assertive, rather self-important unison motif. Ford has decided to visit Falstaff at the Garter under an assumed name (the motif becomes smoother and more insinuating) and set a trap for him. They all swear an oath of secrecy. As they are doing so the women reappear at the back of the stage, and the two ensembles, [8] and [9], are again combined. This time, Fenton stands apart, observing the others and thinking of Nannetta; his vocal line gradually soars free of the rest. The movement works up to a climax, aided by

Luigi Alva (Fenton) with Mirella Freni (Nannetta), an unsurpassed pair of young lovers, at Covent Garden in 1961. (photo: Houston Rogers)

Fenton (Max René Cosotti) steals a kiss from Nannetta (Elizabeth Gale) in Jean-Pierre Ponnelle's 1976 Glyndebourne production, (photo: Guy Gravett)

short, irregularly placed rhythmic figures on brass and drums. Then the men go out, and the women, with their dancing 6/8 metre, are left in the ascendant, rejoicing in the prospect of Falstaff's imminent humiliation. They will blow that great belly up and up till it explodes (thunderous downward chromatic scale on trombones and bassoons). The music clears to a serene E major, the key of the opening, and Alice recites again the extravagant concluding phrase of Falstaff's letter [7]. First Meg and then the other two join in and bring the phrase to a rousing end. There is the same gurgle of melodious laughter. The trumpets take it up in a rapid fanfare, which leads straight into a restatement of the introductory music [5], shortened and this time played out triumphantly by the full orchestra.*

Act Two

Part One: *the interior of the Garter Inn*
The previous scene, with all its hasty comings and goings, was a single unit and, despite its marked lyricism, proceeded at an almost constantly rapid pulse. In contrast, Act Two, Part One is constructed as a series of separate sections, linked and dominated by the commanding figure of Falstaff. We see him, at curtain rise, once more at ease in his armchair, drinking sack. The introductory music, a bounding unison figure ending (twice) in an imperious woodwind trill followed by

*Although the score indicates the same tempo here as the beginning of the scene, there is a tradition going back to Toscanini (and thus presumably sanctioned by Verdi himself) of playing it appreciably faster. The same tradition applies to the orchestral reprise of [15] which ends Act Two, Part One.

a brusque *fortissimo* chord from the whole orchestra, exudes confidence, authority, and a huge appetite for life. Falstaff is in his domain, awaiting events. Bardolph and Pistol appear, full of (feigned) penitence, beating their breasts in time to the music. Their master scarcely bothers to raise an eyebrow: 'villains return to vice like mice to the larder'. There are more urgent matters afoot. And a moment later Bardolph ushers in the first of his visitors. It is Mistress Quickly, who enters curtseying prodigiously [12]. She would like a word with Sir John in private — and the quiet, expectant C major texture of the strings stirs with sly chromatic inflexions on violas and second violins. Falstaff graciously grants her an audience — provoking another profound obeisance (*'Reverenza!'* 'O your Worship!') — and the prying Bardolph and Pistol are ordered out of the room. Even then she can hardly bring herself to speak her delicate message (the violins graphically convey her hesitancy): 'Madonna Alice Ford — alas, unhappy lady!', [13]. What a great seducer he is! Falstaff agrees, but begs her to get to the point. The music begins at last to shed its caution. Jaunty triplet figures are bandied about the orchestra, leading up to the motto which has already been anticipated in Act One and which is to be the rhythmic motif of the opera [14]: *'dalle due alle tre'* — 'from two till three' — the hour when Ford always goes out and his wife, who has received Falstaff's letter and is mad with love for him, can entertain him undisturbed. *'Povera donna!'* repeats Mistress Quickly [13], she has a jealous husband. *'Dalle due alle tre'*, murmurs Falstaff. Then, while the orchestra bounds with delighted expectation, he requests his visitor to convey the message that he will be there. Quickly now turns to the subject of Meg Page; she too — unhappy lady — sends Falstaff the most tender reply, but unfortunately her husband is rarely out of the house (the music changes to a mock-lachrymose *Largo* in 6/8, with sobbing repeated notes and wide-spaced, glistening orchestration). Surely the knight must bewitch them all! No, no witchcraft, answers Falstaff affably, only a certain personal charm. He rewards his 'good she-Mercury' (*'mercuria femina'*) with a coin and, after a final deep curtsey [12], she leaves.

The moment she is gone, Falstaff settles back triumphantly in his chair, while the orchestra crows with satisfaction [15]. Alice is his! 'Jack, go your ways...' (*'Va, vecchio John'*); 'this old capacious body is still preparing new kinds of joy for you'; and to strutting accompaniment on strings, bassoons, brass and timpani he contemplates the splendour of his body. At 'is still' (*'ancora'*), the string flourishes suggest him exultantly wagging his head, and a trumpet tucket evokes the gleam in his eye as he pictures the whole of womankind ready to risk perdition for his sake: 'Good paunch of old Sir John... now you reward me'. His self-congratulations are interrupted by the entry of Bardolph, breathlessly announcing a second visitor — a certain Master Brook (Mastro Fontana) who has brought with him as a gift a demi-john of Cyprus wine. 'Welcome brook that... overflows in such abundance', replies Falstaff, on the crest of his high good humour; 'admit him'. 'Jack, go your ways...', he adds, lost again in his reveries.

Ford enters, in disguise, to a gingerly, angular figure on the violins, full of hesitations which, unlike Mistress Quickly's, are not play-acting but real, telling us plainly how awkward he feels. The watching Bardolph and Pistol comment gleefully that Falstaff is about to fall into Ford's trap (a moment later they are sent packing by a gesture of dismissal); but, as the music shows by its uneasy, twisted figures and sudden violent chords, Ford is very unsure of his role and seems on the verge of giving the game away. The contrast between his embarrassment and Falstaff's self-assurance is emphasised by the genial warmth of the knight's C major greeting, *'Caro, signor Fontana'* ('Dear Master Brook I greet you.') [16],

Ford (Richard Stilwell) listens to Falstaff (Geraint Evans) triumphantly expounding his plans. Covent Garden, 1978. (photo: Clive Barda)

striking grandly across Ford's queasy A major.

Gradually, however, Ford relaxes, helped by a bag of gold which he dangles (with jingling orchestral accompaniment) in front of the interested Falstaff; and at last he comes to the point. He is in love with a lady of Windsor, wife of a certain Ford, called Alice [17]; but try as he will, and lavish gifts on her as he does, she remains indifferent and rebuffs his advances. Ford's narration begins suavely; but fired by his genuine feelings of jealous suspicion about his wife, he warms to his task, and the music rises to an impassioned intensity [18]reminiscent of the great melodic span of Elisabetta's 'Arcan terror m'avea nel cor', the moment in the first Act of *Don Carlos* when she realises that Carlos loves her. Falstaff expresses his sympathy, and together they recall the old song about love giving the lover no peace. But why is Master Brook confiding in him? What can he possibly do to help? To his surprise ('curious request'), Ford asks him to seduce Alice for him, in return for the money he has brought. Alice makes a great point of her chastity (the stabbing offbeat accents of the tortuous melody show us Ford's true feelings underlying his words). If Falstaff like the practised man of the world he is can only break down her defences and pave the way for him, Master Brook can follow. Sir John calmly accepts the commission. He can guarantee success. Master Brook will possess Ford's wife (the assurance prompts a strangled 'Thank you' from Ford). 'In half an hour she'll be in my embraces.' Who? shouts the thunderstruck Ford, nearly betraying himself. 'Alice', is the complacent reply; he has just had word from her that her boor of a husband will be out between two and three. '*Dalle due alle tre*', echoes Ford in a horrified whisper. But Falstaff is too caught up in his vision of conquest to notice. He is going to put horns on that brute: '*Te lo cornifico*' ('I'll horn the buffalo') ([20], a motif related to Quickly's '*Povera donna*'); and, consigning Alice's husband to the devil with his ancestor Menelaus (a rasping augmented triad, with prominent trombones, drums and lower woodwind), he begs Master Brook to excuse him: time is pressing and he must now go (taking the money with him) and make himself beautiful for the assignation.

The whole duet has been set to music of incomparable élan (reflecting every turn and shade of feeling with a power of dramatic invention to which such a short account cannot hope to do justice). Now comes a change, as a motionless string chord, echoing the augmented triad with which Falstaff consigned Ford to the devil, brings the headlong course of the music to a halt. It shows us Ford stunned and uncomprehending. 'Is it a dream?' Slowly the appalling truth sinks in. His wife *is* deceiving him. The horns predicted by Bardolph and Pistol are already sprouting from his forehead. Rouse yourself, Master Ford! 'They dare to tell us that a sensible husband's never jealous!' [21] Yet what could be more humiliating than the whispered gossip, the looks behind one's back? As Ford imagines the horror of it, Falstaff's scornful '*Te lo cornifico*' [20] starts up in the orchestra, answering the throbbing of Ford's tortured brain. He curses marriage; and the orchestra lashes itself into a fury. But they'll not escape! No — he'll catch them at it and be revenged. Ford is now almost sobbing, with [20] drumming insistently in the orchestra. With a final effort he pulls himself together, a great hymn in praise of jealousy rising from low B flat to high G [22]. The full orchestra defiantly roars out the jealous husband theme [21] — only to deflate completely, in a transition as masterly as it is unexpected, as Falstaff re-enters the room to an elegant, slightly mincing theme on the first violins [23]. He is wearing a new doublet and hat and carrying a cane and, all smiles, will not hear of preceding Master Brook out of the door. Ford, gritting his teeth, is equally insistent that Falstaff go first, even though the knight, with an expansive gesture, points out

Geraint Evans as Falstaff and Mario Borriello as Ford dispute who should go first in Carl Ebert's 1958 production, designed by Osbert Lancaster, which was seen both at Glyndebourne and in Paris. (photo: Guy Gravett)

that he is host and, besides, there is no time to waste, the appointment is due. Eventually, after a protracted exchange of courtesies, they link arms and go out together. A reprise of [15], *tutti* and *fortissimo*, brings down the curtain.

Part Two: *a room in Ford's house*
A patter of quavers on first and second violins, as though running on tiptoe, sets the scene. The merry wives have met to hear the result of Mistress Quickly's embassy. She herself hurries in, to a bustling theme that seems to shake with laughter [24], and announces that the trick has taken. When she has caught her breath she recounts her mission, in suitably stately tones [25] — to which the woodwind do not fail to add a sly reminder of the triplet rhythm [14] — and mimicks Falstaff's portly accents and her own deep *'Reverenza'*. But the long and short of it is — and here she breaks into cheerful, perky quavers doubled by piccolo and oboe [26] — that the knight has swallowed the bait, and will be here between two and three. But it is already two, exclaims Alice. The bustling theme [24] resumes as Alice hastily summons her servants to get everything ready, including the big basket of dirty linen, which they are later to empty into the river. Then she notices Nannetta's woebegone expression. The poor girl tearfully explains, in a poignant B minor, that her father wants to marry her to Dr Caius. What! That 'buzzard', that 'dullard'? Never! Her tears duly dried, they make ready for the great moment, imagining the impact the laundry basket will make when it hits the water and discharges its colossal contents (massive unisons from top to bottom of the orchestra). The opening tiptoe music returns, with

Tito Gobbi as the fat knight going courting at Covent Garden. (photo: Donald Southern)

delightfully realistic pauses for thought as Alice makes the final arrangements — a chair here, the screen open there, a lute placed on the table: the comedy is about to begin!

The rhythm changes to a lilting, laughing 6/8 and a captivating tune sung by Alice, then taken up by Nannetta and Meg as well, celebrates the happy comradeship, high spirits and jests of the merry wives [27]. Mistress Quickly watches at the window for Falstaff's arrival. A moment later: 'There he is'; and the music winds down rapidly through a succession of quiet but tense string chords and falling woodwind arpeggios. Meg, Nannetta and Quickly have just time to go to their posts and Alice to sit at the table and, taking up the lute, strum a few chords, before Falstaff is upon her. He enters eagerly, murmuring a snatch of song to the lute (guitar in the orchestra): 'At last I pluck thee, my fragrant blossom', then places a hand on Alice's bosom and draws her to him. She gets to her feet, laying down the lute; and the orchestral strings steal in with a soft but ardent sequence of chords whose rich suspensions speak of more than simple play-acting. The whole passage maintains a marvellously fine balance between comedy and passion, beauty and absurdity. Falstaff's affectation of the bluff, honest fellow without affectations may be accompanied ironically by a comical bassoon, Alice's 'O soave Sir John!' ('O enchanting Sir John!') may be sung knowingly to the rhythm of 'dalle due alle tre'; but there is unfeigned intensity of desire in those string suspensions, and not only Falstaff's own imagination but, for a fleeting instant, Alice's, is captured in spite of herself by his vision of her as his 'Lady', brilliantly attired and shining with jewels. Her vocal line seems to fall momentarily under the spell of his, when it exactly echoes the phrase to which, in the first scene of the opera, he praised Ford's wife for her surpassing beauty. Falstaff is beginning to press her close when Alice deflects him by a gentle allusion to his bulk, whereupon he is moved to recall the far-distant days when he was a page, and conjures out of the air a sparkling image of himself as a youth: 'Quand' ero paggio del Duca di Norfolk' [28]*. The text of this appropriately diminutive aria — the solitary example of a self-contained number in the entire opera — is inspired by Falstaff's words in Henry IV, Part One: 'When I was about thy years I was not an eagle's talon in the waist, I could have crept into any Alderman's thumb-ring', and the music is as light and glinting as thistledown.

For a moment Falstaff has lost himself in admiration of his own conceit. Alice brings him down to earth. How can she trust him not to deceive her when he loves another — Meg? Falstaff brushes the idea aside contemptuously. It is Alice he loves, and he cannot wait a thousand years to hold her in his arms. Just in time Mistress Quickly enters (as arranged) in a great bustle of (assumed) agitation: Meg is on her way there, and in a rare state. The tempo speeds up abruptly, and a busy theme in semiquavers vividly suggests the ordered scurry as the next stage of the merry wives' plot begins [29]. Falstaff hides behind the screen just as Meg, choking back her laughter, enters crying that Ford suspects that Alice has a man hidden in the house and is coming to cut his throat. Alice plays up with a terrified 'Misericordia' (fortissimo chord of B flat complete with memorable cymbal clash). A moment later Quickly rushes in genuinely alarmed: Ford is coming, he's already in the garden with a whole crowd of people behind him, yelling murder! A new theme takes over, faster and less controlled, announced by the second violins, and running up and down the scale like wild fire [30]. Ford's voice is heard nearby, shouting threats and orders. Alice closes the screen round Falstaff so as to hide him completely, and turns to face Ford. He abuses her ('rea moglie') then

*The aria lasts thirty seconds. Victor Maurel, the first Falstaff, in a famous studio recording, sang it three times — the last in French — and it still only takes a minute and a half.

'Falstaff' at Sadler's Wells in 1949; Tyrone Guthrie's production featured Arnold Matters in the title role, Orwen Price as Quickly, Marion Lowe as Alice, and Anna Pollak as Meg. (photo: Angus McBean; Harvard Theatre Collection)

Josephine Veasey, Mariella Angioletti, Regina Resnik and Geraint Evans as Falstaff. (photo: Keystone Press Agency Ltd)

hands his keys to Dr Caius, telling him to search the house and open everything, and himself rummages frenziedly in the laundry basket, flinging dirty washing about the room. Foiled by the empty basket, he storms out. Alice goes out by another door to look for her servants (and is offstage and thus unaccounted for during the action which follows). As soon as Ford has left, Meg helps Falstaff to squeeze into the laundry basket (he is now swearing that he loves her alone) and piles some of the washing back on top of him. Unseen by any one, Nannetta leads Fenton behind the screen, where they embrace; for the space of a few bars the music settles into a serene, luminous E flat major, with snatches of the now distant hubbub [30] playing about the charmed circle. Then [30] returns *fortissimo* in G major as Bardolph and Pistol encounter Ford and Caius, still shouting like men possessed. They have found nothing. Suddenly, in a momentary silence, the sound of kissing is heard from behind the screen. All stop dead, then slowly, fingers to their lips, led by Ford, advance on the screen. Meg and Quickly, by the basket, pretend to busy themselves with the laundry. Within the screen the young lovers, blissfully oblivious, continue their endearments. The resultant ensemble — one of the high points of the comedy and a necessary interlude of slower tempo in a scene of rapid action — is composed of very diverse elements: the whispered, half stifled threats of the men, the laughing triplets of the women, the quiet but momentous *pizzicato* of the strings, the groans of Falstaff from within the buck-basket ('I'm stifling!. . . I'm choking!. . . Please help me!') and the soaring lyrical phrases of the lovers. At last: 'one. . . two. . . three' — the attackers reach the screen and hurl it to the ground. Consternation! ('*Sbalordimento!*'). Ford rages: has he not told Fenton a thousand times that Nannetta is not for him? An instant later Bardolph and Pistol call out that Falstaff has been seen on the stairs. 'Dismember him!', yells Ford, and to an excited restatement of [30], *fortissimo*, the whole crowd pours out in pursuit. Immediately Alice, who had entered, unseen, in time to witness the débâcle of the screen, summons her servants: 'Ned, Will, Tom, Isaac!' The men struggle with their mighty load (great heaving unisons on the full orchestra), and stagger with it to the window. There is a pause; horn tremolos picture the basket teetering on the window ledge. Then '*Patatrac!*' With an immense orchestral explosion, an avalanche of strings and a crowing fanfare of trumpets, the basket hits the water. Ford, re-entering bemused, is led by his wife to the window to join in the general laughter at the spectacle of Sir John Falstaff, festooned with dirty linen, floundering in the Thames.

Act Three

Part One: *a yard. To the right the outside of the Garter Inn, with the inn sign and its motto 'Honi soit qui mal y pense', and a bench by the doorway. It is sunset.* The scurrying theme in semiquavers [29] associated in the previous scene with the beginning of Falstaff's humiliations starts low down in the strings like a mutter of distant thunder, then gradually rises through the whole orchestra to a hammering *fortissimo* as the curtain rises to reveal the knight seated, deep in gloomy thought. With a brief imperious gesture (bright A major chord followed by sweeping violin semiquavers) he pounds the table and summons the landlord, then relapses into his black humour. '*Mondo ladro. Mondo rubaldo.*' ('A bad world, I say. A villainous world.') His sombre conclusions are punctuated by a limping, dragging unison figure of repeated notes on trombones, horns and lower woodwind, petering out with a kind of depressed shake of the head [31]. The monologue is based on *The Merry Wives* ('Have I lived to be carried in a

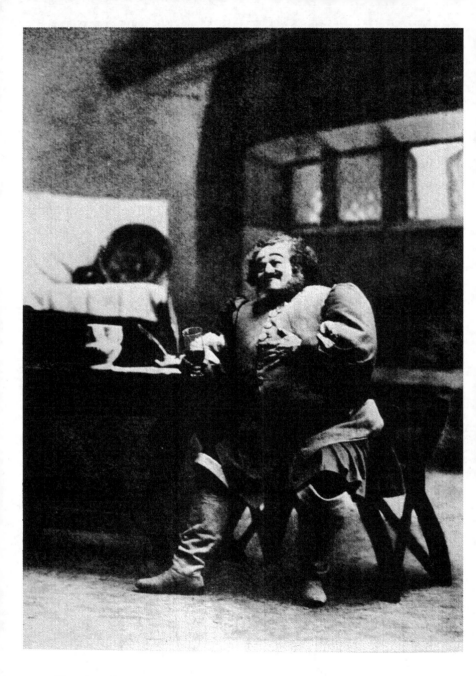

Victor Maurel as Falstaff. Maurel created the role and sang it in New York and London in 1895. (Mander and Mitchenson Theatre Collection)

Geraint Evans in the title role — Covent Garden, 1978. (photo: Donald Southern)

basket, like a barrow of butcher's offal, and to be thrown into the Thames?'), enriched by the grander egoism of *Henry IV, Part One*. At the memory of his recent degradation the orchestral texture stirs into indignant life. How near he came to a dirty death! Ugh! how water swells a man; and there is a sympathetic gurgle on the horns, rising in a violent *crescendo* as though spewing it up in disgust. He returns to his dark meditations [31]. The orchestra begins a shrugging, listless minor-key version of *'Va, vecchio John'* [15]: 'Go thy ways old Jack; if manhood, good manhood be not forgot on the face of earth'. The music warms momentarily into a proud D flat major, only to fade into silence. A whisper of [29] returns, in the minor. But here is the innkeeper, bringing mulled wine in a large beaker (repeat of the bright chord and scale in A major). At once his gloom is forgotten. 'I'll send this friendly potion to join the Thames inside me.' He sips, smacking his lips, then drinks deeper, unbuttoning his waistcoat. The violas graphically trace the downward progress of the wine. Still more vivid is the warmth of the glowing C major chord that spreads over the strings (supported by octave horns) as Falstaff utters a contented *'Buono'* ('That's good'). Under its reviving influence he is moved to a disquisition on the genial properties of wine, how it disperses melancholy and little by little sets a man's whole being a-quiver with life: until the whole orchestra is one vast, vibrant trill.

His delight is cut short in full spate by an all too familiar voice: *'Reverenza'* [12]. Falstaff whirls round and sees Mistress Quickly curtseying deeply. In a volley of abuse he denounces Alice and all her works: for her treacherous sake he has been almost suffocated, melted like a pat of butter, plunged hissing hot in the Thames. Quickly is unperturbed and pacifies him with smooth explanations, blaming the wretched servants. Alice — unhappy lady [13] — is red-eyed with weeping. She has written him a letter. Falstaff is hooked again. He takes the letter — watched by Alice, Meg, Nannetta, Ford, Dr Caius and Fenton, who peep in turn round the corner of a house opposite the tavern — and reads it aloud: 'I shall wait for you at midnight in Windsor Park. You must come disguised as Herne, the Sable Huntsman and at Herne's Oak I shall meet you'. 'Love loves a mystery', explains Quickly; Alice is using 'a strange old Windsor tale' to see him again. They go inside to discuss it in private. As they leave, Mistress Quickly begins telling him of the legend of Herne who hanged himself from the Oak and who has been seen to walk there. When they have gone, the conspirators come forwards, congratulating themselves. Alice, to the eerie accompaniment of horns and piccolo, takes up the tale of the Sable Huntsman, in a perfect parody of Verdi's 'sinister' manner, with soft, shuddering tremolo, writhing chromatic lines, clarinets in the bottom register, the lurid gleam of sustained brass chords, and the dull thud of the bass drum. Meg and Nannetta confess that they feel really frightened. Alice laughingly replies, to a dancing theme of the utmost gaiety [32], that it is only a fairy-tale invented to make children go to sleep. But a mood of genuine enchantment has begun to settle over the music; from this point onwards it will intensify, with the gradual onset of darkness, in preparation for the final scene.

When Alice mentions the long horns sprouting from the huntsman's head, Ford cannot restrain a satisfied 'Bravo! When I see those huge antlers I'll enjoy them!' 'Careful', answers his wife; 'you should be punished too. Daring to doubt your wife!' They all make plans for the masquerade, to the sound of soft strings and a gentle ripple of woodwind arpeggios. Nannetta, in white dress and veil with a band of pink at the waist, will be Queen of the Fairies, Meg Nymph of the Woods, and Mistress Quickly a witch; a group of children will dress up as imps and elves (a gleeful, light-fingered tune in D minor [33]), and they'll all set on the fat knight and make him atone for his wickedness.

'Falstaff' at Sadler's Wells (1949) with Arnold Matters. (photo: Angus McBean; Harvard Theatre Collection)

Regina Resnik as Mistress Quickly (Met. Archives)

In the fading light the women and Fenton disperse to make ready. Ford and Caius remain. Mistress Quickly, coming unobserved out of the inn, overhears Ford's plan for the doctor to marry Nannetta [34] (the music is a kind of prosaic, four-square version of [32]). Caius will recognise her by her white dress with pink at the waist, and at the end of the revels Ford will bless them as man and wife (unctuous string harmonies which, in the light of what is to come, sound comically self-satisfied). As they go off Mistress Quickly comments: 'Don't be certain!' Appropriately, [34], now in 3/4 time, undergoes a magical transmogrification, feathering lightly down through the dusk. The stage is now empty. Distant voices call to one another: 'Be ready with that fairy song I taught you!' 'I know it well.' 'And don't be late.' The orchestra, first with the imps' theme [33], then with [34] rising through the instruments like a spark of light in the darkness, has the last mysterious word.

Part Two: *Windsor Park, with Herne's great oak tree. It is night.*
The horn-calls of the park rangers are heard in the distance. As Fenton, first to arrive, steps into the clearing, the woodwind recall the love music from Act One [10]. His ecstatic love-song [35] (whose shimmering texture includes, for the first time in the opera, a harp) ends by quoting the magical *'Bocca baciata'* [11]. As before, it is answered by Nannetta, who hastens towards him. Their kiss is interrupted by Alice. No time for that now! They must work fast if Ford's plan is to be foiled. To the accompaniment of a light, high-spirited figure on the strings (derived from [1]), Alice and Nannetta dress Fenton in a monk's black robe and cowl and a mask — the same disguise that Dr Caius will be wearing. Who is going to impersonate the bride, asks Alice? 'A rascally red-nosed knave', replies Quickly (to an echo of [24] in the violins).

At the sound of heavy steps they hide in the undergrowth. Falstaff, wrapped in a capacious cloak, with a pair of antlers strapped to his head, enters the glade, to a solemn motif on the strings which contrives to suggest both the absurdity and the mysterious enchantment of the scene [36]. A distant clock strikes. Falstaff, standing by the oak, counts the chimes, while the string harmonies stir beneath the repeated note of the bell like the secret life of the nocturnal forest itself. It is midnight. The strings repeat [36] several times, softly, then broaden into sonorous chords as Falstaff reflects that even Jove took on the likeness of a bull for love of his Europa.* A soft footfall is heard. It is Alice, his own love! He attempts to embrace her. He is her stag! They are alone together at last! No, whispers Alice, Meg has followed her through the wood. Well, he will have them both: let them tear him in two like a roasted buck and each take a haunch! The orchestra's rapid heart-beat (two-note *staccato* figures alternating between upper and lower strings and woodwind) has increased to a violent hammering of unison strings and timpani and triumphant brass; Falstaff is in no mood to be trifled with. But at that moment Meg's voice is heard, calling in alarm: 'The wicked goblins!' 'For all my sins may Heaven forgive me!', cries Alice, and disappears. Falstaff drops to the ground with a bump at the foot of Herne's Oak. From the wood comes the sound of a voice (Nannetta's) summoning the elves and sprites. Falstaff throws himself face downwards. At once the glade is peopled with fairy shapes. Alice arranges

*Cf. *'Tutto è tranquillo e placido'* in the last act of *The Marriage of Figaro*, where Figaro, himself (as he supposes) about to 'wear the horns', invokes classical mythology, in music that marks a similar moment of contemplation between passages of rapid tempo —one of several interesting parallels between the final scenes of the two operas. See my essay in *Responses*, p. 27 and n. *Secker & Warburg* 1973.

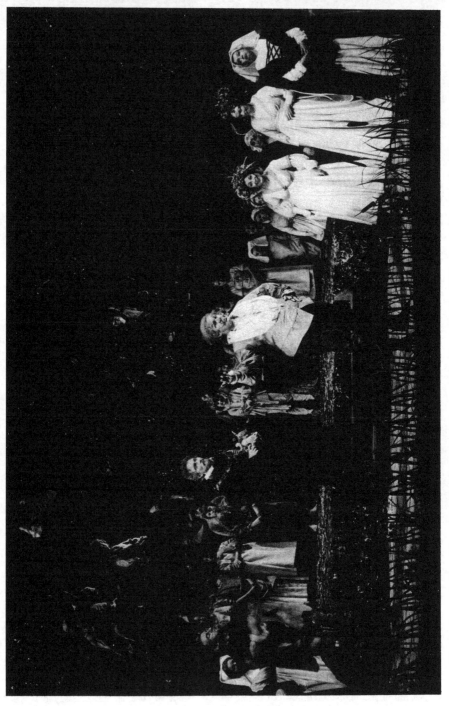

The final scene in Jean-Pierre Ponnelle's 1976 Glyndebourne production with Donald Gramm in the title role. (photo: Guy Gravett)

them in their order, and the children group themselves in a circle round their Queen.

Verdi now summons his subtlest orchestral skills for an evocation of the moonlit park and the glimmering forms gliding and weaving about in it: harp and divided violins, the soft skirl of woodwind, the glow of horns, and riding above them Nannetta's high clear voice, inviting her fairies to the dance; whereupon, the music's gentle 3/4 changes to an even more enchanted common-time, a serene high-stepping dance accompanied by quiet chords on harp, horns and strings.

The whole company of fairies and sprites and goblins has been moving slowly towards the oak tree. Suddenly Bardolph (dressed in a monk's habit but without a mask) stumbles against Falstaff's prostrate body. An angry cry goes up: a man! And horned like a bull, round as a pumpkin, huge as a ship! And corrupt, impure! We'll do an exorcism, shouts the 'monk'. Under cover of the ensuing bustle, Alice whispers to Nannetta to take care: Dr Caius is looking for her. Alice and Mistress Quickly conceal her from view and hurry her and Fenton off into the wood.

The tormenting of Falstaff now begins. Children jump all over him and roll his body about on the ground. Sting him, pinch him, stick him and prick him, command the merry wives, to an appropriately piquant chromatic theme [37] accompanied by *pizzicato* violins and violas and triangle. The men join in. As the drubbing, verbal and physical, gathers ferocity, the metre changes from 6/8 to 2/4 and the orchestration grows fuller and the accentuation heavier. A braying, hee-haw motif, which has been heard in various forms throughout the opera (usually in connection with Falstaff's or Ford's humiliation), lends emphasis to the rich abuse heaped on the recumbent knight. The blows become more violent still, each sequence of blows being marked by an entry a semitone higher, with trumpets and trombones attacking the new note *fortissimo* a beat before the voices. 'Domine fallo casto' ('Chasten his spirit, Lord we pray'), cry the women piously (in a parody of religious music which echoes the 'Hostias' in Verdi's *Requiem*). But save his belly ('l'addomine'), replies Falstaff, punning irrepressibly. For, even at this lowest ebb of his fortunes, his wit has not deserted him. And when Bardolph, in the excitement of the moment, lets his cowl fall back, exposing his face, the tormented man, springing up with a mighty cry of 'Riconosco Bardolfo!' (in his own home key of C major), turns on his tormentor, unleashing a torrent of abuse on that ignoble 'ignis fatuus', that depraved 'salamander'.

This final effort has exhausted him, however; he must pause for breath (the violas and cellos quietly repeating the hee-haw figure). While the others applaud ironically, Mistress Quickly draws Bardolph to one side: 'Come now. It's time to don your bridal garments.' They disappear, unnoticed, under the trees. Well, Sir John, asks Ford, stepping forward, which of us is the one with the horns? 'Caro Signor Fontana', replies the unabashed Falstaff, in the same genial C major in which he greeted his visitor in Act Two [16]. No, interposes Alice, this is Ford, my husband. More loud laughter in the orchestra. Before Falstaff can recover from his astonishment, he hears a mocking 'Cavaliere' [12], and sees Mistress Quickly giving a low bow — which he acknowledges with a grimace and a ceremonious 'Reverenza'. She proceeds to rub in the lesson. What on earth made him imagine that two women would ever dream of giving themselves to a fat, sweaty old man like him? The whole company join in and jeer unmercifully. But Falstaff, with that resourcefulness in adversity which is one of his chief glories, now rises from the ruins of defeat. He may have made an ass of himself (another hee-haw, on oboes, bassoons and violas). But without him, for all their jeering and their cocksureness they would be dull and savourless. It is he and he alone ('son io' repeated three times with a grandly swelling inflexion) that makes them clever.

He is not only witty in himself but the cause that wit is in other men — the last words sung to a phrase of marvellously elegant effrontery [38].

The third act of *Falstaff* is sometimes criticised as an anticlimax, the mere duplication of what has already taken place in the second. But this is to overlook two crucial points. First, it is necessary that Falstaff be made everybody's butt, and that his humiliation seem complete, so that the unquenchable spirit of the man may be fully demonstrated. In the end, his incorrigible 'imagination', which Mistress Quickly and the others have ridiculed, refuses to yield to the superior common sense of the rest of the world. Secondly, the two conspiracies differ in one essential respect. In Act Two Ford believes that his wife is deceiving him. In Act Three, realising that she isn't, and having been let into the new plot against Falstaff, he assumes that this time he is fully aware of what is going on, and while busy making an ass of Falstaff makes a bigger ass of himself.

The moment of revelation is at hand. 'Now the Queen and her bridegroom are advancing' announces Ford, as Dr Caius leads a veiled Queen of the Fairies by the hand. An exquisite minuet strikes up gently on flutes and strings, at once serenely classical and with a sly air of butter-wouldn't-melt-in-its-mouth [39]. And here is another pair of lovers seeking a blessing on their betrothal, adds Alice, introducing Fenton, masked, and Nannetta, concealed beneath a blue veil. Ford affably admits them to the rites and pronounces a blessing on both couples. 'May heaven unite you. . . Now remove the disguises. Apotheosis!' Loud laughter. 'Disaster!' 'Who betrayed me?', shout Caius and Ford almost together. 'Fenton with my daughter!' 'I am married to Bardolph!' 'A man is sometimes caught in a trap that he himself has prepared for others', replies Alice (to yet another characteristic merry wives' melody). Once again Falstaff steps forward: '*Caro buon Messer Ford*' [16], 'who's now been fooled?' Ford has the grace to laugh, and resigns himself to the inevitable. Falstaff recommends a chorus to round off the scene (an excited fanfare from the trumpets). And Ford invites everyone to dinner with Sir John, perhaps thinking of the large bag of money that Falstaff had off him earlier in the day. There is a rousing call to order by the whole orchestra, unison — appropriately, to a variant of the hee-haw motif. Then Falstaff launches the famous fugue — '*Tutto nel mondo è burla*' (All the world's a jest) [40]. When Fenton takes up the theme in the dominant, Falstaff replies with a countersubject derived from the ubiquitous '*dalle due alle tre*' motif. The fugue — Boito's 'mighty burst of laughter' — works up, with immense energy and good humour, to a climax, breaking off dramatically on a diminished seventh chord. After a silence, Falstaff, alone and unaccompanied, utters a slow, mock-tragic '*Tutti gabbati*/ (lit. 'everyone's gulled'). '*Tutti gabbati*', reply the others dolefully, as though a sudden cloud were passing over the face of the sun. The cloud goes as swiftly as it came, the tempo recovers, there is a rapid *crescendo*, the vocal ensemble culminates in an immense uprush of high spirits, and the opera ends as it began, with a great orchestral flourish in C major.

(a) *Act One, scene one*

FALSTAFF

Must on oc - ca - sion fal - ter
De - vo ta - lor da un la - to

(b) *Act One, scene two*

ALICE

a cou - ple true and ten - der
in un a - mor ri - deri - te

(c) *Act Two, scene one*

FALSTAFF

From the mo - ment we met
Vo - glio fa - re con voi

(d) *Act Three, scene two*

THE FAIRY QUEEN

Marking the beat with gen - tle feet
Le magiche ac - cop - pian - do

(e) *Act Two, scene two*

FALSTAFF

My love - ly A - lice!
Mia bel - la A - li - ce!

(f) *Act Three, scene one*

ALICE

Long be - fore it's mor - ning,
pria che il ciel rag - gior - ni,

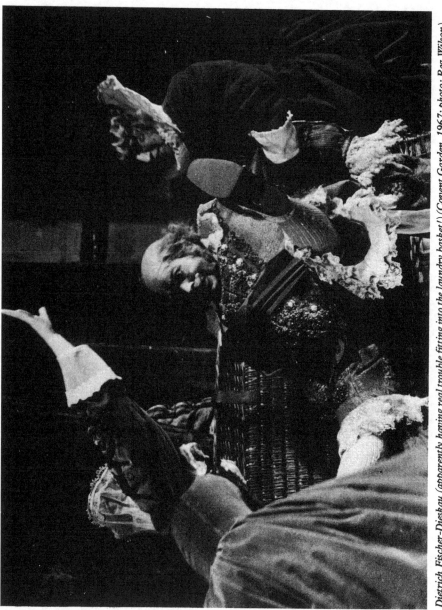

Dietrich Fischer-Dieskau (apparently having real trouble fitting into the laundry basket!) (Covent Garden, 1967; photo: Reg Wilson)

Translating 'Falstaff'

Andrew Porter

Soon after the Scala première of *Falstaff*, Boito wrote to his friend the French critic Camille Bellaigue: 'Where shall I begin?... You cannot imagine the immense intellectual joy that this Latin lyric comedy produces on the stage. It's a real outpouring of grace, of strength, and of gaiety. Shakespeare's sparkling farce is led back by the miracle of sound to its clear Tuscan source, to 'Ser Giovanni Fiorentino' [i.e. Boccaccio]. Come, come dear friend, to hear this masterpiece; come to spend two hours in the gardens of the *Decameron*.' To 'Ser Giovanni', with the date 1378, was attributed the collection of fifty tales called *Il pecorone*, published in 1558; the first novella presents a lover who, like 'Master Brook', fell in love with another's man's wife and 'many a time sent to her messages and gifts, but she took no heed of these'. The second is the 'clear Tuscan source' of Shakespeare's *Merry Wives*. (The first novella of the Fourth Day is the source of *The Merchant of Venice*.)

Three points in Boito's letter should be stressed. First, *Falstaff* (unlike *Il barbiere* and *Don Pasquale*; that implication becomes clear elsewhere in the letter) is an Italian opera buffa that can provide intellectual joy. Second, it is not only graceful and gay but also strong. I forego an encomium on the musical marvels, melodic, instrumental, and structural, which *Falstaff* contains in order to dwell on the third point, most relevant to a translator. In mentioning Boccaccio's *Decameron*, Boito was to some extent praising his own contribution to the opera – to what extent I realized when reading the *Decameron* in an edition published in Venice in 1552. At the end, the editor, Girolamo Ruscelli, has compiled a 'Vocabolari generale di tutte le voci usate dal Boccaccio, bisognose di dichiaratione...'. Among the words deemed needful of explanation are *nacchere, cozzare, aizzare, strozzare, ruzzare, rintuzzare, scrollare, punzecchiare* and several others that reappear in Boito's and Verdi's *Falstaff*. In adapting Shakespeare, Boito employed a vocabulary that even in mid-16th-century Italy — before Shakespeare was born — was thought to need glossing. And there is an even closer Boccaccian connexion. While he was preparing the libretto, Boito wrote to Verdi:

> The love between Nannetta and Fenton must appear in frequent bursts. Whenever they are present, they'll exchange kisses, hidden in corners, cunningly, ardently, without being discovered, with fresh little phrases and brief, stealthy, very rapid little dialogues, from the beginning to the end of the comedy.... It will be a lively, merry love, always disturbed and interrupted, always ready to start again.... As one sprinkles sugar on a tart, so I should like to sprinkle the whole comedy with this merry love, not have it all collected together at one point.

As the motto of this lively, merry love, Fenton and Nannetta sing the recurrent lines *Bocca baciata non perde ventura, Anzi rinova come fa la luna* ('A kissed mouth doesn't lose its freshness, for like the moon it renews itself'), and they are worked into the (Petrarchan, not Shakespearean) sonnet that opens the final scene. These lines come from the *Decameron*, where — with rather different import —they end the Seventh Story of the Second Day: the story of a woman who, despite the fact that eighty different men had made love to her on thousands of occasions, nevertheless entered her husband's bed as a virgin and convinced him that she really was one'. The *Decameron* had reached Henry IV's England. Chaucer rendered some of the tales into English. In my *Falstaff* translation, I have left the two lines untranslated. One might presume that an Italian copy of the *Decameron* had got into Fenton's hands. While he couldn't quite have been educated at Eton, for that school was not founded until about thirty years after the time of *Falstaff*, he perhaps knew enough Italian to puzzle out the sense of the words that he and Nannetta, in all innocence, adopt as their catchphrase. The lines were still celebrated in 19th-century England; Rossetti (as James Hepokowski has noted) entitled his portrait of Fanny Cornforth 'Bocca baciata'. But the real

Giacomo Rimini as Falstaff (Stuart-Liff Collection)

reason for leaving them untranslated is: *luna* must plainly be *moon*, to retain the gentle shine of the sustained *u/oo* vowel as Verdi set it; one can try *charm* or *enchant* for the important *-cia-* of *baciata*; but it seems to be impossible to surround that moon with any words that both make sense and sound right. In all five of the previous *Falstaff* translations I know, the charm of the enchanting melody has been lost. But let me stress that this recurrent quotation, thrown into musical prominence, is a special case: not the thin edge of a wedge that would drive apart the solid reasons for doing such an opera as *Falstaff* in the language of the artists and the audience, not licence for regularly leaving the untranslatable untranslated!

Shakespeare's Falstaff says 'Let the sky rain potatoes'. The precise Boito, knowing that nearly two centuries had to pass before Sir Walter Raleigh's colonists brought their potatoes back from what is now North Carolina, changed them to truffles. I have reinstated the pleasant anachronism. Otherwise, I have tried to balance on that tightrope that any translator of a Shakespeare opera must tread, one where an attempt to impose the English original on music made to other words often leads to a topple. But in this respect at least *Falstaff* was easier to tread than *Macbeth*. Boito handled the Bard more freely than Piave and Maffei did; he used fewer 'well-known quotations'. Most of the time only translation, not 'back-translation', was called for. I tried in an English version to catch and match so far as possible the spirit of the comedy as Boito and Verdi perceived it, and also to share in the fun they both had when playing pranks with metre and rhyme. Most of Falstaff's scenes are written in long 'fourteeners':

> *So che se andiam, la notte di taverna in taverna,* (Act One, 1)

or: *Versiam un po' di vino nell'acqua di Tamigi,* (Act Three, 1)

or: *Questa è la quercia. Numi proteggetemi! Giove!* (Act Three, 2)

It evidently amused Boito to break them up at times, as in this Pistol/Dr Caius exchange from the first scene:

> *Gonzo!*
>   *Pezzente!*
>   *Bestia!*
>   *Can!*
>   *Vil!*
>   *Spauracchio!*
>   *Gnomo!*
> *Germoglio di mandragora!*
>   *Chi?*
>   *Tu.*
>   *Ripeti!*
>   *Sì.*

And it evidently amused Verdi, who from the start of his career had exhorted his various librettists to escape the strict metrical conventions and formulas ('the more novel and bizarre the forms, the better'), to conceal rhymes, to oppose a poetic metre with a different musical metre, to make verse sound like freely declaimed prose, to expand fourteen syllables into as many as seventeen or eighteen (by putting rests between two vowels that in poetic scansion are elided to count as one). The translator must follow the music. My English lines do not scan with the smooth accuracy of Boito's. But the surprising enjambments are often his, and in Mistress Quickly's narration:

> I drop a curtsey, bending very low be-
> Fore him: my confidential message follows

is not a misprint but a representation of the way Boito achieved a rhyme with *posa:*

> *E a lui m'inchino molto ossequiosa-*
> *mente, poi passo alle notizie ghiotte.*

Falstaff's wooing of Alice includes the passage:

> *Nell'iri ardente e mobile dei rai*
> *Dell'adamante,*
> *Col picciol piè nel nobile*
> *Cerchio d'un guardinfante*
> *Risplenderai*
> *Più fulgida d'un ampio arcobalen*

(literally: 'In the blazing, shimmering rainbow of the diamond rays, with your little foot in the noble circle of a farthingale, you will shine more splendidly than a broad rainbow').

This is a very free expansion of Shakespeare's 'I see how thine eye would emulate the diamond. . .and the firm fixture of thy foot would give an excellent motion to thy gait in semicircled farthingale'.

The first, third and fifth lines illustrate Boito's play of inner rhyme and end rhyme. I've found the passage variously translated as:

1. I see you now, sweet Alice, your eyes
   Gleaming with pleasure,
   Your cheeks aglow with happiness
   When you behold my treasure.
   All the world will bow
   Before you in joy and delight.

2. With golden chains entwining thy tre-
   Sses of gold still brighter,
   And on thy white neck shining
   Pearls that are scarcely whiter,
   Thy dazzling eyes
   Like lamps of love fresh lit by Cupid's flame.

3. O brighter than the diamond, those eyes
   Late on me rested!
   I'd robe thee WITH attire of gold,
   Thy locks with pearls invested:
   Thy splendour I'd
   Redouble so thou shouldst appear a right rainBOW!

4. You gentle FE-MI-NINity, ex-
   Uding its magic power,
   A wondrous new divinity,
   Rare as a blooming flower,
   Illuminates
   The universe, bedazzled by your glow.

5. The rainbow of its radiance, the spar-
   KLE of its diamonds,
   And then your rustling crinolines,
   PROclaim your royal presence.
   Your shining crown
   Shall scintillate resplendent as the sun.

Verdi adds a musical comma after *mobile*, which makes (2) impossible. The second line is at once joined to the first by an enjambment of sense and yet divided from it by a new phrase mark: one needs a translation that allows the singer to dwell on a strong word with a long vowel, corresponding to *rai*, and then catch up the sense with the new phrase of the second line, 'articulating' though not actually breathing. (1) and (3) allow that; (2), (4), and (5) do not. The third line must run straight into the fourth, as Boito's epithet does into his noun; in (3) it cannot. The fourth line breaks the basic pattern by starting with a strong beat; this rules out the *PROclaim* of (5) and makes the emphatic *THY* of (3) rather awkward. The fourth syllable of the first line (*arDENte*) should be able to carry a slight emphasis, which lies awkwardly on the *than* of (3), the *fe* of (4), and the *of* of (5). By typographical devices I have tried to indicate some other things that are surely bad fits: the sustained crotchets on the *fe* and *mi* of *femininity* in (4); the fact that the third line of (3) is likely to be heard as *I'll robe thee with a tyre of gold*. (2), which is the earliest *Falstaff* translation (W. Beatty Kingston's, published by Ricordi in the year of the première) is the only one to get at all close to Boito's complete rhyme scheme.

The example is cited to illustrate the particular preoccupations that guided my own translation: an insistence that long and short, strong and weak, hard and soft, open and closed, bright and dark, heavy and light, joined and discrete, should match the original as closely as is compatible with intelligibility. Verdi's notes can be forced to fit all the lines quoted above. What those lines don't fit is Verdi's music with the phrasing and the inflexions that an Italian singer singing the original would naturally give them. And with increasing fervour I believe that, since the details of Verdi's vocal lines usually have their specific starting point in the words, it is essential that not just the metre and the sense but also the shape and the sound of the original phrasing and the original words should be reflected in the new language, if the music is to live. Not just phrases but individual words within those phrases should press forward, pause, end as they do in the original; otherwise the articulation goes wrong, the singers are not happy, and the audience declares that 'opera in English sounds awful'. When Verdi composes, in effect:

> *Sol al veder*
> *Il Cavalier*
> *Nel guazzo*

it cannot adequately be rendered as

> And when he sees
> Poor Falstaff sad-
> Ly soaking

or: I think he'd like
      To know that we've
      Been joking.

or: Seeing his rye-
      Val in this sad
      Condition.

At the same time, a translation should translate; (1), (2), and (4) above are surely too far from what Boito wrote. All five omit Alice's little foot. My attempt is:

> Those dazzling rays encircle you, their blaze
> Your charms revealing.
> From gold-encrusted farthingale
> Two tiny feet come stealing,
> And you will shine
> More gloriously than any rainbow ever seen.

Gold-encrusted, rather strong for *nobile*, was chosen to provide the stress points and attacks the music requires. The next lines echo an image of Sir John Suckling's which once met can never be forgotten:

> Her feet beneath her petticoat,
> Like little mice, stole in and out.

There is more stress on *two* than I like, and there are other inexactitudes of length and weight that I regret: *ever seen* is mere metrical filling. All the same, I think this version comes a little closer to Boito's imagery than do the others, and I hope it is not too bad a fit for Verdi's music.

All translation is a matter of compromise and of deciding what can least harmfully be sacrificed: sense, sound, rhyme, articulation, phrasing. And it is a matter of making a separate decision almost measure by measure. Sometimes a rhyme may be essential, even if it leads to forced diction. Sometimes — more often — the sound of a particular note is all-important. Sometimes what matters most is to convey a piece of information clearly and dramatically. Something is always lost — but the gain in immediacy, in communication, in vividness outweighs it. Verdi, like most great opera composers, thought it wrong for an audience to sit through a drama performed to an uncomprehending audience; in the first year of its existence, *Falstaff* was published in Italian, English, German, and French.

The first edition of the vocal score had already been published when Verdi made some cuts in the second-act finale (involving new composition) and recomposed the end of Act Three Scene One. This translation follows the revised version. It includes an optional extra word and extra note for Meg—her 'Yes' in reply to Alice's 'Will you provide the lanterns?' A 'Si' was there in the first version, and Verdi, who turned a page at this point as he penned the correction sheets, *may* simply have forgotten to write it in. Boito divided his orginal libretto into numbered scenes, and although the numeration was removed when the work was published, the 'changes of scene' (i.e. of characters concerned, not of décor) are still indicated in the original libretto by bold type initial listing of the characters who appear in each of them. This has been reproduced. The distinct 'scenes' of this apparently continuous opera—reflected in the musical periods and in the harmonic structure—are most clearly indicated in Act Three, where a short double-rule (in the first published libretto, and again in this English edition) as well as the bold-type listing regularly divides them. The stage directions are Boito's, amplified by those found in Verdi's autograph score in a few places where his lively theatrical sense dictated more visual detail than his librettist had provided. Brackets enclose a few directions where I have added to Boito's words some of my own to indicate how the passages fit together in performance.

Thematic Guide

Many of the themes from the opera have been identified in the articles by numbers in square brackets, which refer to the themes set out on these pages. The themes are also identified by the numbers in brackets at the corresponding points in the libretto, so that the words can be related to the musical themes.

[1]

Allegro vivace

[2]

Un poco meno animato (Allegro vivace)

[3] FALSTAFF

Moderato
legato

Allegro

Night after night we wan - der,
So che se an-diam, la not - te

[4]

Moderato

[5]

Allegro vivace

brillante

etc.

Andante sostenuto

Allegro

Your ra- diant glan - ces will shine on me with love
eil vi- so tu - o su me ri-splen-de - rà

Più moderato (Allegro)

That wine He's like a bar-rel, that ap- pa-rel
That monster! -skin! built mountain of blub-ber in kni-ghtly
-ce,chi -co -ra le ciance del bel vag-heg - gi-no
Quel-l'o-tre!quel ti-no! Quel Re del-le pan- ha an-

Più moderato (Allegro)

DR CAIUS   BARDOLPH
He's a vil-lain, he's a van-dal. Fal-staff, as you heard me tel - ling
E un ri-bal-do,un fur-bo un la-dro.Fal-staff si, ri- pe- to giu - ro

Allegretto

dolciss.

N
F
Lips that are bur - ning! Kis - ses that charm me!
Lab - bra di for - co! Lab - bra di fio - re!...

Piu lento (Allegretto)

'Bo- cca ba - cia - ta non per -de ven - tu - ra...'

Assai moderato

Oh your wor - ship!
Re - ve - ren - za!

[13] QUICKLY

Allegro moderato

Un - hap - py la - dy!
Po - ve - ra don - na!

[14] QUICKLY

Allegro moderato

from two till three
dal - le due al - le tre

[15]

Allegro sostenuto

[16] FALSTAFF

Allegro moderato

Dear Ma - ster Brook I greet you!
Ca ro si - gnor Fon - ta - na!

[17] FORD

Andante

In Wind-sor there's a la - dy, love - ly and bright and charm - ing;
C'e a Wind-sor u - na da - ma, bel - la e leg - gia - dra mol - to,

[18] FORD

Andante *poco string.*
legato
con espress.

On her I spent my for - tune, a thou - sand gifts I gave her,
Per lei spre-cai te - so - ri, git - tai do - ni su do - ni

[19] FORD

Allegro moderato *allarg.*

Tho' I may woo in vain I know that all her cold-ness springs from her sense of pride.
Quel - la cru-del bel - ta sempre e vis - su - ta in gran-de fe - de di ca - sti - ta.

Agitato

I'll   horn the buff-a-lo,   will - y   nill - y!
Te   lo   cor - ni - fi - co   net - to   net - to!

[21] FORD

con espansione

They dare   to   tell us   that a sen-si-ble hus-band's ne-ver jea - lous!
E poi   di - ran - no .. che un ma-ri-to ge - lo-so e un in-sen -sa - to!

[22] FORD

Molto più lento (Allegro agitato)

O jea-lous heart I thank you,   my eyes are blind no more —you'll not de - ceive   me.
Lau-da - ta sem-pre si - a   nel fon-do del mio cor — la ge-lo-si - a.

[23]

Molto più lento (Allegro agitato)

[24]

Allegro brillante

[25] QUICKLY

Andante

I   sal - ly   forth un - til I reach the Gar   -   ter
Giun - ta all'Al - ber - go del - la Giar - ret - tie   -   ra

[26] QUICKLY

Allegro

So he, to put it brief - ly, be - lieves you two   la – dies
In – fin, per far - la spic - cia, vi cre - de en - tram — be

[34]

Allegro

pp

[35] FENTON

Andante assai sostenuto

dolcissimo

From lo - ver's lips a tender song is stea - ling; thro' the sha-dows how ar-dent-ly it flies on;
Dal la-bbro il can-to e-sta-si-a - to vo-la... pei si - len-zi not-tur-ni e va lon-ta - no

[36]

Andante sostenuto

poco dim.   *pp*

[37] ALICE

Prestissimo

pp

Pri-cke-ty,   pri-cke-ty, pri-cke-ty, pro-cke-ty, sti-cke-ty, sti-cke-ty, sti-cke-ty, sto-cke-ty,
Piz-zi-ca,   piz-zi-ca, piz-zi-ca, stu-zzi-ca, spi-zzi-ca, spi-zzi-ca, pun-gi, spil-luz-zi-ca,

[38] FALSTAFF

Moderato

dolce

wits   some
And thanks to   my   wit   your   can find em - ploy - ment
L'ar - gu - zia   mi - a   cre - a l'ar - gu-zia degl 'al - tri

[39]

Allegretto

dolce

[40] FALSTAFF

Allegro brioso

pp legg.

world's
All in the   but   fol - ly. Man   is born to be jol - ly, is born to be jo - lly.
Tut-to nel mon-do è   bur - la. L'uom   e na-to bur-lo-ne, bur - lo-ne, bur - lo - ne.

58

Falstaff

A comic opera in three acts

Music by Giuseppe Verdi

Libretto by Arrigo Boito after

Shakespeare's *The Merry Wives of Windsor* and *Henry IV*

English translation by Andrew Porter

Falstaff was first performed at the Teatro alla Scala, Milan, on February 9, 1893. It was first performed in London at Covent Garden on May 19, 1894 and in America at the Met. on February 4, 1895.

This translation was commissioned by Sarah Caldwell and first performed at the Orpheum Theater, Boston, on February 5, 1975.

The numbers in square brackets refer to the Thematic Guide.

CHARACTERS

Sir John Falstaff	*baritone*
Ford *Alice's husband*	*baritone*
Fenton	*tenor*
Dr Caius	*tenor*
Bardolph ⎫ *Falstaff's retainers*	*tenor*
Pistol ⎭	*bass*
Mistress Alice Ford	*soprano*
Nannetta *Alice's daughter*	*soprano*
Mistress Quickly	*mezzo-soprano*
Mistress Meg Page	*mezzo-soprano*
The Host of the Garter Inn	
Robin *Falstaff's page*	
A little page of Ford's	

Townspeople and Country people – Ford's Servants
A Masquerade of imps, fairies, witches, etc.

Act One

Part One. *Inside the Garter Inn. A table. A large armchair. A bench. On the table, the remains of a meal, numerous bottles and a glass. Inkpot, pens, paper, a lighted candle. A broom leaning against the wall. Exit at the back, a door on the left.*

Falstaff, Dr Caius, Bardolph, Pistol, the Innkeeper in the background

Falstaff is busy heating sealing-wax in the flame of the candle: then he seals two letters with a ring. After sealing them, he extinguishes the flame and starts drinking, comfortably stretched out in the armchair. [1]

DR CAIUS
(entering by the door at the left, with a threatening shout)

Falstaff! Falstaff!

FALSTAFF
(paying no attention to Dr Caius's outburst, calls to the innkeeper, who approaches)

Mine host! Olà!

DR CAIUS
(louder than before)

Sir John Falstaff!! Sir John Falstaff!!

BARDOLPH
(to Dr Caius)

Why are you shouting?! Oh! che vi piglia?!

DR CAIUS
(still shouting, and approaching Falstaff, who pays no attention to him)

You have beaten my servants! Hai battuto i miei servi! . . .

FALSTAFF
(to the innkeeper, who goes out to fulfill his order)

Landlord! pray bring me Oste! un'altra bottiglia
A new flask of sherry. Di Xeres.

DR CAIUS
(as before)

And you rode my best horse Hai fiaccata la mia giumenta baia,
till it was winded,
And broke into my dwelling. Sforzata la mia casa.

FALSTAFF

But left your cook in safety. Ma non la tua massaia.

DR CAIUS

That was generous! She's an ugly old Troppa grazia! Una vecchia cisposa. Ampio
baggage. Hear me, Sir Falstaff, Messere,
Though twenty-five times over you bore Se foste venti volte John Falstaff Cavaliere
that knightly title,
I mean to make you answer me. Vi sforzerò a rispondermi.

FALSTAFF
(calmly)

Well you may have my answer: [2] Ecco la mia risposta:
'I did those things you speak of'. Ho fatto ciò che hai detto.

DR CAIUS

And so? E poi?

FALSTAFF

And I enjoyed them. L'ho fatto apposta.

DR CAIUS
(yelling)

To the King's Council I shall appeal. M'appellerò al Consiglio Real.

FALSTAFF

Heaven go with you!   Vatti con Dio.
They'll laugh you out of England. Better   Sta zitto o avrai le beffe; quest'è il consiglio
  accept my counsel.   mio.

DR CAIUS
(turning his fury on Bardolph)

I have not done yet!!   Non è finita!

FALSTAFF

Go hang yourself!   Al diavolo!

DR CAIUS

You, Bardolph!   Bardolfo!

BARDOLPH

Worthy Doctor.   Ser Dottore.

DR CAIUS
(in a threatening tone)

Last night you set me drinking.   Tu, ier, m'hai fatto bere.

BARDOLPH

Too deeply! How I regret it!   Pur troppo! e che dolore! ...
(inviting Dr Caius to take his pulse)
I'm ill. I wish you'd diagnose my sickness. Sto mal. D'un tuo pronostico m'assisti.
  All my insides   Ho l'intestino
Are ruined. Accursed landlord, who mixes   Guasto. Malanno aglo osti che dan la calce
  lime with sherry!   al vino!
(laying his forefinger on his enormous, rubicund nose)
See this red, blazing meteor?   Vedi questa meteora?

DR CAIUS

I see it.   La vedo.

BARDOLPH

         Why does it shine   Essa si corca
So fiery and red in the darkness?   Rossa cosi ogni notte.

DR CAIUS
(exploding)

        I diagnose the gallows!   Pronostico di forca!
You made me drink, you ruffian, with him   M'hai fatto ber, furfante, con lui
(pointing to Pistol)
        while telling stories;   narrando frasche;
When I'd had far too much to drink emptied Poi, quando fui ben ciùschero, m'hai
  my pockets.   vuotate le tasche.

BARDOLPH
(with dignity)

Not I.   Non io.

DR CAIUS

Then who?   Chi fu?

FALSTAFF
(calling)

Eh, Pistol!   Pistola!

PISTOL
(coming forward)

My master.   Padrone.

FALSTAFF
(still seated in the armchair)

        Could it be you, sir,   Hai tu vuotate
Who picked the doctor's pockets?   Le tasche a quel Messere?

DR CAIUS
(turning his wrath on Pistol)

Sure, it was him. Observe him!   Certo fu lui. Guardate

See how his ugly features attempt in vain to hide it!

Come s'atteggia al niego quel ceffo da bugiardo!

(turning a pocket of his doublet inside-out)

This pocket had two shillings of Edward's reign inside it,

Qui c'eran due scellini del regno d'Edoardo

And six florins of silver. Now not a coin is left me.

E sei mezze-corone. Non ne riman più segno.

PISTOL
(to Falstaff, brandishing a broom with dignity)

Sir John, may I defend myself and wield this wooden weapon?

Padron, chiedo di battermi con quest' arma di legno.

(to the doctor forcefully)

You are lying!

Vi smentisco!

DR CAIUS

You ruffian! Insult a man of breeding!

Bifolco! tu parli a un gentiluomo!

PISTOL

Blockhead!

Gonzo!

DR CAIUS

You beggar!

Pezzente!

PISTOL

Coward!

Bestia!

DR CAIUS

Dog!

Can!

PISTOL

Scum!

Vil!

DR CAIUS

You scarecrow!

Spauracchio!

PISTOL

Frenchie!

Gnomo!

DR CAIUS

You offspring of mandragora!

Germoglio di mandràgora!

PISTOL

Who?

Chi?

DR CAIUS

You.

Tu.

PISTOL

Repeat that!

Ripeti!

DR CAIUS

Yes!

Si.

PISTOL
(hurling himself at Dr Caius)

By thunder!!!

Saette!!!

FALSTAFF
(restraining Pistol with a gesture)

Hey there! Good Pistol, don't fire your shots indoors.

Ehi là! Pistola! No scaricarti qui.

(calling Bardolph, who approaches)

And Bardolph! Tell me who picked the pockets of the doctor?

Bardolfo! Chi ha vuotato le tasche a quel Messere?

DR CAIUS
(breaking out)

One of the two did.

Fu l'un dei due.

BARDOLPH
(calmly pointing to Dr Caius)

He was drinking, fell in a stupor,	Costui beve, poi pel gran bere
Drank till he lost his senses; now he tells you a fable,	Perde i suoi cinque sensi, poi ti narra una favola
A tale he dreamed while he lay snoring under the table.	Ch'egli ha sognata mentre dormi sotto la tavola.

FALSTAFF
(to Dr Caius)

Mark that. And when you've marked it well, the truth has been revealed you.	L'odi? Se ti capaciti, del ver tu sei sicuro.
The charges stand refuted. So you may leave in peace.	I fatti son negati. Vattene in pace.

DR CAIUS

Mon dieu!	Giuro.
If again I should feel the need to go a-drinking,	Che se mai mi ubbriaco ancora all'osteria
I'll drink with honest people, sober, pious and godly.	Sarà fra gente onesta, sobria, civile e pia.

(Exit by the door at the left.)

BARDOLPH *and* **PISTOL**
(clownishly accompanying Dr Caius as far as the door, and chanting)

AMEN!	AMEN!

FALSTAFF

Cease the antiphony. Your wailing has no rhythm.	Cessi l'antifona. La urlate in contrattempo.

(Bardolph and Pistol stop and draw close to Falstaff.)

Stealing should be like counterpoint: achieved with charm and in tempo.	L'arte sta in questa massima: "Rubar con garbo e a tempo".
You are inferior artists.	Siete dei rozzi artisti.

(He begins to examine the bill which the innkeeper has brought with the bottle of sherry.)

6 pullets: 6 shillings.	6 polli: 6 scellini;
30 flagons of sherry: 2 pounds. 3 turkeys ...	30 giare di Xeres: 2 lire; 3 tacchini ...

(to Bardolph, throwing him the purse, and then proceeding with his careful examination of the bill)

See what money is left me. Two pheasants. One anchovy.	Fruga nella mia borsa. – 2 fagiani. Un'acciuga.

BARDOLPH
(tipping the change out onto the table and counting it)

A mark, a mark, a penny.	Un mark, un mark, un penny.

FALSTAFF

Search.	Fruga.

BARDOLPH

I have searched.	Ho frugato.

FALSTAFF

Search harder!	Fruga!

BARDOLPH
(throwing the purse down on the table)

There, not a farthing left in it.	Qui non c'è più uno spicciolo.

FALSTAFF
(rising)

You will be my destruction!	Sei la mia distruzione!
Ten pounds a week it costs me to sustain you! You drunkard!	Spendo ogni sette giorni diechi ghinee! Beone!
Night after night we wander, trying tavern [3] after tavern,	So che se andiam, la notte, di taverna in taverna,
And your blazing nose lights up my path, and serves me as a lantern!	Quel tuo naso ardentissimo mi serve da lanterna!

But what I save in tallow you squander in the tavern.　　Ma quel risparmio d'olio tu lo consumi in vino.

(calmly)

Thirty years I've replenished that nose of yours and kept it shining! You're not worth it.　　Son trent'anni che abbevero quel fungo porporino! Costi troppo.

(to Pistol)

You're no better!　　E tu pure.

(to the innkeeper, who is still there, and then goes out)

Landlord! A bottle of sherry!　　Oste! un'altra bottiglia.

(turning back to Bardolph and Pistol)

You consume all my substance! If Falstaff should grow slender, He'd not be me, then who would love me? My paunch proclaims me, [4] He who sees it acclaims me, and Sir Falstaff names me!　　Ni struggete le carni! Se Falstaff s'assottiglia Non è più lui, nessun più l'ama; in quest'addome C'è un migliaio di lingue che annunciano il mio nome!

PISTOL
(cheering)

Falstaff enormous!　　Falstaff immenso!

BARDOLPH
(likewise)

Tremendous Falstaff!　　Enorme Falstaff!

FALSTAFF
(patting and regarding his belly)

This is my glory. I'll make it grow! – Have done now, our wits have to sharpen.　　Quest'è il mio regno. Lo ingrandirò. Ma è tempo d'assottigliar l'ingegno.

BARDOLPH and PISTOL

Sharpen away.　　Assotigliam.

(all three in a huddle)

FALSTAFF

Do you know a certain man in Windsor Whose name is Ford?　　V'è noto un tal, qui del paese Che ha nome Ford?

BARDOLPH

Yes.　　Sì.

PISTOL

Yes.　　Sì.

FALSTAFF

A man of wealth and substance ...　　Quell'uomo è un gran borghese ...

PISTOL

They say he's rich as Croesus.　　Più liberal d'un Creso.

BARDOLPH

A Lord!　　È un Lord!

FALSTAFF

His wife is lovely.　　Sua moglie è bella.

PISTOL

And holds the purse-strings.　　E tien lo scrigno.

FALSTAFF

Precisely! Ah love! Starry her glances! Swanlike her neck! Her lips? A flower, a smiling blossom! Her name is Alice, and one day as I went by she saw me, And gazed full on me, smiling. And lightning struck from her eyes At my heart. The fiery glances flashed from the goddess, falling full　　È quella! O amor! Sguardo di stella! Collo di cigno! e il labbro? Un fior! Un fior che ride. Alice è il nome a un giorno come passar mi vide Ne' suoi paraggi, rise. M'ardea l'estro amatorio Nel cor. La Dea vibrava raggi di specchio ustorio

65

On me, on me, on sturdy shoulder, on stalwart bearing,	Su me, su me, sul fianco baldo, sul gran torace,
On shapely leg, on splendid figure, manly, capacious;	Sul maschio piè, sul fusto saldo, erto, capace;
And her desire so plainly matched the love that I was feeling,	E il suo desir in lei fulgea si al mio congiunto
That she seemed to say: "I'm yours, Sir John Falstaff".	Che parea dir: "Io son di Sir John Falstaff".

BARDOLPH

Period.   Punto.

FALSTAFF
(taking up Bardolph's interruption)

New sentence. Another . . .   E a capo. Un'altra . . .

BARDOLPH, PISTOL

Another!   Un'altra!

FALSTAFF

And this one's name is Mistress Margaret.   E questa ha nome: Margherita.

PISTOL

They call her Meg.   La chiaman Meg.

FALSTAFF

She has also felt the charm of John Falstaff.	È anch'essa de'miei pregi invaghita.
And she too has the holding . . .	È anch'essa tien le chiavi . . .

ALL THREE

. . . of the purse-strings.   . . . dello scrigno.

FALSTAFF

So these two	Costoro
Shall be my mines of plenty and my Eldorado!	Saran le mie Golconde e le mie Coste d'oro!
Behold me, my fruitful autumn is an Indian summer,	Guardate. Io sono ancora una picente estate
Love is in season. So here, two letters filled with passion.	Di San Martino. A Voi, due lettere infuocate.

(He gives Bardolph one of the two letters which have been lying on the table.)

You take this note to Meg; her virtue shall be tried.	Tu porta questa a Meg; tentiam la sua virtù.

(Bardolph takes the letter.)

I see that fiery nose gleams with excitement.	Già vedo che il tuo naso arde di zelo.

(He hands the other letter to Pistol.)

And you,   E tu
Bear this note to Mistress Alice.   Porta questa ad Alice.

PISTOL
(refusing it with dignity)

I bear the sword of knighthood.	Porto una spada al fianco.
I'll not play Master Pandarus. Beneath me.	Non sono un Messer Pandarus. Ricuso.

FALSTAFF
(with calm disdain)

Lazy scoundrel.   Saltimbanco.

BARDOLPH
(advancing, and throwing down the letter on the table)

Sir John, in this endeavour I cannot be of help to you.	Sir John, in quest'intrigo non posso accondiscendervi.
I'm barred by . . .	Lo vieta . . .

FALSTAFF
(interrupting)

What?   Chi?

BARDOLPH

My Honour.   L'Onore.

FALSTAFF
(seeing the page Robin who enters upstage)
Hey! Robin!   Ehi! paggio!
(suddenly, to Bardolph and Pistol)
You two go hang yourselves   Andate a impendervi,
But not on me!   Ma non più a me.
(to the page, who then runs out with the letters)
Two letters here, take them, to these two   Due lettere, prendi, per due signore.
ladies:
And take them quickly. Hurry! Run!   Consegna tosto, corri, via, lesto, va!
Hurry! Run!
Hurry, go, go, go, go, go!   Lesto, va, va, va, va, va!
(turning back to Pistol and Bardolph)
Your Honour!   L'Onore!
Scoundrels! You dare to stand upon your   Ladri! Voi state ligi all'onor vostro, voi!
honour, you!
You dare to talk of honour when I myself,   Cloache d'ignominia, quando, non sempre,
yes I,   noi
Must sometimes pawn my honour! John   Possiam star ligi al nostro. Io stesso, sì, io,
Falstaff, I, I, I,   io,
Must on occasion falter, hoping that God   Devo talor da un lato porre il timor di Dio
won't see me,
And in a time of need dispense with honour,   E, per necessità, sviar l'onore, usare
descend
To using half-truths and strategems, trim   Stratagemmi ed equivoci, destreggiar,
my sails, use evasions.   bordeggiare.
But you, you ragged beggars with shifty   E voi, coi vostri cenci e coll'occhiata tórta
glances, squinting
Like cross-eyed polecats, with smiles and   Da gatto-pardo e i fetidi sghignazzi avete a
dirty sniggers, you prate of honour,   scorta
You boast of that! What's honour? What's   Il vostro Onor! Che onore?! che onor? che
that? What's that? What's honour?   onor? che ciancia!
I'll tell you! Can this honour feed a man   Che baia! Può l'onore riempirvi la pancia?
when he's hungry?
No. Can this honour mend a leg that's   No. Può l'onor rimettervi uno stinco? Non
broken? It can't.   può.
An ankle? No. A finger? No. Or a whisker?   Né un piede? No. Né un dito? No. Né un
No.   capello? No.
For honour's not a surgeon. What is it? Just   L'onor non è chirurgo. Che è dunque? Una
an expression.   parola.
And what is in this expression? Just a   Che c'è in questa parola? C'è dell'aria che
wandering vapour.   vola.
Fine expression! This honour, can it be felt   Bel costrutto! L'onore lo può sentir chi è
by a dead man?   morto?
No. Thrives it with the living? By no means: No. Vive sol coi vivi? . . . Neppure: perché
a flattering word can   a torto
Convert it into folly, and by pride it's   La gonfian le lusinghe, lo corrompe
corrupted,   l'orgoglio,
By slander it's infected. As for me, I'll not   L'ammorban le calunnie; e per me non ne
have it. No!   voglio! No!

But getting back to you two scoundrels,   Ma, per tornare a voi, furfanti, ho atteso
I've been too patient,   troppo,
And I dismiss you.   E vi discaccio.
(He takes the broom and pursues Bardolph and Pistol, who dodge the blows by taking refuge under the table.)
Be off! Hurry! Hurry! At a gallop!   Olà! Lesti! Lesti! al galoppo!
At a gallop! To the hangman who waits for   Al galoppo! Il capestro assai bene vi sta.
you there!

Villains! Leave my sight! Leave my sight!   Ladri! Via! Via di qua! Via di qua! Via di
  Leave my sight!   qua!
(Bardolph escapes by the door at left. Pistol makes for the exit upstage, but not without a buffet or two from Falstaff, who pursues him.)

Part Two. *A garden. Ford's house on the left. Clumps of trees in the centre of the stage.*

Alice, Nannetta, Meg, Mistress Quickly, then Ford, Fenton, Dr Caius, Bardolph, Pistol.

Enter Meg and Mistress Quickly from the right. They cross to Ford's house, and at the door they meet Alice and Nannetta who are coming out. [5]

MEG
(greeting her)

Good Alice.   Alice.

ALICE
(greeting her)

Meg.   Meg.

MEG
(greeting her)

Nannetta.   Nannetta.

ALICE
(to Meg)

        I hoped to find you,   Escivo appunto
To share a joke with you.   Per ridere con te.

(to Quickly)

      Good day, Dame Quickly.   Buon di, comare.

QUICKLY

May God make you merry.   Dio vi doni allegria.

(stroking Nannetta's cheek)

    And you, my rosebud.   Botton di rosa!

ALICE
(again to Meg)

Happy encounter!   Giungi in buon punto.
For I'll surprise you, I have news to tell you.   M'accade un fatto da trasecolare.

MEG

So have I.   Anche a me.

QUICKLY
(who was talking to Nannetta, approaches with curiosity)

Eh?   Che?

NANNETTA
(also approaching)

    What is it?   Che cosa?

ALICE
(to Meg)

      Tell me your story.   Narra il tuo caso.

MEG

Tell me yours.   Narra il tuo.

NANNETTA *and* **QUICKLY**

    Tell us, tell us.   Narra, narra.

ALICE
(to all of them, in a huddle)

      But swear you'll   Promessa
Not breathe a word.   Di non ciarlar.

MEG

You know me?   Ti pare?

68

Oho! You know me!   Oibò! Vi pare?!

ALICE

Well then: if I were tempted to leave the straight   Dunque: se m'acconciassi a entrar ne'rei
And narrow path of piety, then I   Propositi del diavolo, sarei
Could gain a title, be a titled lady!   Promossa al grado di Cavalleressa!

MEG

Me too!   Anch'io.

ALICE

You're jesting.   Motteggi.

MEG
(*She hunts in her pocket and draws out a letter.*)

Then let me show you;   Non più parole,
In black and white I can prove what I'm saying.   Chè qui sciupiamo la luce del sole.
I have a letter here.   Ho una lettera.

ALICE
(*hunting in her pocket*)

I also.   Anch'io.

NANNETTA *and* QUICKLY

Oh!!   Oh!!

ALICE

Read it.   Leggi.
(*She gives the letter to Meg.*)

MEG
(*She gives Alice her letter in exchange.*)

Read it.   Leggi.
(*reading Alice's letter*) [6]
"Wonderful Alice! How I love you . . ."   "Fulgida Alice! amor t'offro . . ."
What's this?   Ma come?
Can I believe it?   Che cosa dice?
Except for the name,   Salvo che il nome
The same beginning.   La frase è uguale.

ALICE
(*reading the letter addressed to Meg*)

"Wonderful Meg! How I love you . . ."   "Fulgida Meg! amor t'offro . . ."

MEG
(*continuing to read Alice's letter*)

". . . and desire you."   ". . . amor bramo."

ALICE

Here "Meg", there "Alice".   Qua "Meg", là "Alice".

MEG

Otherwise equal.   E tal e quale.
(*She continues reading.*)
"Oh, do not ask me why, but say you . . ."   "Non domandar perché, ma dimmi: . . ."

ALICE
(*continuing from her letter*)

". . . love me."   ". . . t'amo."
I gave him no cause   Pur non gli offersi
To hope.   Cagion.

MEG

We're in a   Il nostro
Strange situation.   Caso è pur strano.

(*All in a group. comparing the letters word for word, handing them to each other with curiosity.*)

QUICKLY

Let's take things calmly.   Guardiam con flemma.

MEG

The same expressions.   Gli stessi versi.

ALICE

Identical paper.   Lo stesso inchiostro.

QUICKLY

Very same writing.   La stessa mano.

NANNETTA

Everything matches.   Lo stesso stemma.

ALICE *and* **MEG**
(together, each reading from her own letter)

"You are merry and charming, and I am   "Sei la gaia comare, il compar gaio
    spry and
Disarming, so, as you see we'd make a fine   Son io, e fra noi due facciamo il paio."
    pair."

ALICE

Well!   Già.

NANNETTA

He, she, you.   Lui, lei, te.

QUICKLY

A pair of three!   Un paio in tre.

ALICE

"We'd make a fine pair, a couple true and   "Facciamo il paio in un amor ridente
    tender
(their noses buried in the letters)
A lovely lady, a man . . ."   Di donna bella e d'uom . . ."

ALL

". . . of knightly splendour . . ."   ". . . appariscente . . ."

ALICE

"Your radiant glances will shine on me   [7] "E il viso tuo su me risplenderà
    with love,
Shine like the starlight, like a shining star   Come una stella sull'immensità."
    in heaven above."

ALL
(laughing)

Ha! Ha! Ha! Ha! Ha! Ha! Ha! Ha!   Ah! Ah! Ah! Ah! Ah! Ah! Ah! Ah!

ALICE
(finishing the letter)

"Your servant waits to hear,   "Rispondi al tuo scudiere,
John Falstaff, Cavalier."   John Falstaff, Cavaliere."

ALL

Monster!   Mostro!

ALICE

He must be punished.   Dobbiam gabbarlo.

NANNETTA

And taught a lesson.   E farne chiasso.

ALICE

We'll mock him at our leisure.   E metterlo in burletta.

Oh! Oh! We'll fool him!   Oh! Oh! che spasso!

QUICKLY

It's a duty!   Che allegria!

MEG

It's a pleasure!   Che vendetta!

(*Alice, Quickly, Meg and Nannetta sing their opening lines in the following ensemble in a series of overlapped entries. Then they all start at the beginning again, singing simultaneously. Each addresses now one, now another, chattering in a group.*)

ALICE

Preposterous wine-skin!	[8] Quell'otre! quel tino!
He's built like a barrel,	Quel Re delle pance,
That mountain of blubber	Chi ha ancora le ciance
In knightly apparel.	Del bel vagheggino.
That man must be seventy,	E l'olio gli sgocciola
He ought to know better	Dall'adipe unticcio
Than write that impertinent,	E ancor ei ne snocciola
Importunate letter!	La strofa e il bisticcio!
I'll change into curses	Lasciam ch'ei le pronte
His amorous spluttering,	Sue ciarle ne spifferi;
His mouthing and muttering	Farà come i pifferi
Of lovestricken verses.	Che sceser dal monte.
Just wait till we punish you	Vedrai che, se abbindolo
And make you obey,	Quel grosso compar,
For all your impertinence,	Più lesto d'un guindolo
John Falstaff, you'll pay.	Lo faccio girar.

MEG

A strange sort of tempest	Un flutto in tempesta
In Windsor has blown up!	Gittò sulla rena!
Instead of a Jonah,	Colui, se l'abbraccia,
The whale has been thrown up!	Ti schiaccia Giunone.
A whale that is amorous,	Ma certo si spappola
Presumptuous and daring,	Quel mostro al tuo cenno
But we mean to capture him,	E corre alla trappola
Our trap we're preparing.	E perde il suo senno.
We'll strike him and spear him,	Potenza d'un fragile
Our tongues are sharp lances.	Sorriso di donna!
We'll melt all his blubbery	Scïenza d'un'agile!
With fire from our glances.	Movenza di gonna!
When we set our claws in him	Si el vischio lo impegola
He won't get away!	Lo udremo strillar,
Oh, when we advance on him	E allor la sua fregola
For mercy he'll pray!	Vedremo svampar.

NANNETTA

If sport you're preparing	Se ordisci una burla,
I hope I can share it.	Vo'anch'io la mia parte.
He'll pay for his daring,	Conviene condurla
I swear it, I swear it.	Con senno, con arte.
A snare we must lay for him	L'agguato ov'ei sdrucciola
And craftily hide it.	Convien ch'ei non scerna;
He won't guess what's happening	Già prese una lucciola
Until he's inside it.	Per una lanterna.
We must not be hasty	Che il gioco rïesca
When we spring our trap on him,	Perciò più non dubito;
To capture him suddenly,	Per coglierlo subito
Our bait must be tasty.	Bisogna offrir l'esca,
We'll snare him with flattery	E se i scilinguagnoli
And catch him today,	Sapremo adoprar,
We'll baste him and batter him	Vedremo a rigagnoli
And melt him away.	Quell'orco sudar.

That man is a cannon!	Quell'uomo è un cannone!
And women excite him.	Se scoppia, ci spaccia.
Beware the explosion	Di Windsor codesta
If passions ignite him.	Vorace balena.
All Windsor is blown up	Ma qui non ha spazio
Unless we defuse him,	Da farsi più pingue;
So we must be clever,	Ne fecer già strazio
And catch and accuse him.	Le vostre tre lingue.
Our tongues are sharp arrows	Tre lingue più allegre
When we set them clattering	D'un trillo di nacchere,
And chirping and chattering	Che spargon più chiacchiere
Like six broods of sparrows.	Di sei cingallegre.
Beware of our merriment,	Tal sempre s'esilari
For we'll make you pay.	Quel bel cinguettar.
Take care when the merry wives	Così soglion l'ilari
Of Windsor are gay!	Comari ciarlar.

(*They move off.*)

(*While the women are going off to the left, from the right* **Master Ford, Dr Caius, Fenton, Bardolph** *and* **Pistol** *make a lively entrance. Ford is at the centre of the group, with Pistol on his right, Bardolph on his left, and Fenton and Dr Caius behind him. Clustered together, the four other men address Ford sotto voce, urging their complaints. From time to time during the earlier part of the men's ensemble, some or other of the women are glimpsed through the trees at the back, unnoticed by the men, and they repeat some phrases of their earlier ensemble; then they disappear altogether. The five men, simultaneously, sing the verses below.*)

DR CAIUS
(*to Ford*)

He's a villain, he's a vandal,	[9] È un ribaldo, un furbo, un ladro,
He's an out-and-out barbarian;	Un furfante, un turco, un vandalo;
In my house he made a scandal	L'altro di mandó a soqquadro
That obese octogenarian.	La mia casa e fu uno scandalo.
And I mean to set the law on him,	Se un processo oggi gl'intavolo
Yes, a lawsuit I'm intending.	Sconterà le sue rapine.
It would make a worthy ending	Ma la sua più degna fine
If the devil laid his claw on him.	Sia d'andare in man del diavolo.
But those villains who stand beside you,	E quei due che avete accanto
They're as bad as him or worse,	Gente son di sua tribù.
Though they prate about their virtue	Non son due stinchi di santo
They're the men who stole my purse.	Né son fiori di virtù.

BARDOLPH
(*to Ford*)

Falstaff as you heard me telling —	Falstaff, sì, ripeto, giuro,
You will find it barely credible —	(Per mia bocca il ciel v'illumina)
I repeat, John Falstaff meditates	Contro voi John Falstaff rumina
An assault upon your dwelling.	Un progetto alquanto impuro.
I'm a man of shining virtue,	Son uom d'arme e quell'infame
I'm a man of sensitivity.	Più non vo' che v'impozzangheri;
I'd not stoop to such activity	Non vorrei, no, escir dai gangheri
Though a kingdom should reward me.	Dell'onor per un reame!
Master Ford, you heard my warning	Messer Ford, l'uomo avvisato
Of the trick that he has planned.	Non è salvo che a metà.
Up to you to trick the trickster	Tocca a voi d'ordir l'agguato
And obtain the upper hand.	Che l'agguato stornerà.

FORD
(*first to himself and then to the others*)

Like a swarm of hornets hovering,	Un ronzio di vespe e d'avidi
They are buzzing all around me;	Calabron brontolamento,
Like the howling of a hurricane,	Un rombar di nembi gravidi
All these voices just confound me.	D'uragani è quel ch'io sento.
Four are speaking all together,	Parlan quattro ed uno ascolta;
Not a sentence can be heard!	Qual dei quattro ascolterò?
If you wouldn't speak together	Se parlaste uno alla volta
I might understand one word!	Forse allor v'intenderò.

PISTOL
(to Ford)

All your happy days are ended,	Sir John Falstaff già v'appresta,
Master Ford, beware calamities!	Messer Ford, un gran pericolo.
For above your head suspended	Già vi pende sulla testa
I can see the sword of Damocles.	Qualche cosa a perpendicolo.
Master Ford, I know his wickedness,	Messer Ford, fui già un armigero
Day and night I could observe him;	Du quell'uom dall'ampia cute;
As you see, I'm truly penitent	Or mi pento e mi morigero
That I ever stooped to serve him.	Per ragioni di salute.
Now you know that danger threatens,	La minaccia or v'è scorperta,
So beware that bloated rake.	Or v'è noto il ciurmador.
On your guard, be on your guard, sir!	State all'erta, all'erta, all'erta!
For your honour is at stake.	Qui si tratta dell'onor.

FENTON
(to Ford)

You may count upon my readiness	Se volete, io non mi perito
To reduce the knight to reason	Di ridurlo alla ragione
With a word or two in season,	Colle brusche o colle buone,
Or a blade of perfect steadiness.	E pagarlo al par del merito.
With a puncture anatomical,	Mi dà cuore mi solletica
I could prick that swollen belly,	(E sarà una giostra gaia)
Or reduce that flesh to jelly;	Di sfondar quella ventraia
I will find that highly comical.	Iperbolico-apoplettica.
With advice or with a sabre	Col consiglio o colla spada
If I meet him face to face,	Se lo trovo al tu per tu,
I can send the man to heaven,	O lui va per la sua strada
Or perhaps that other place.	O lo assegno a Belzebù.

FORD
(to Pistol)

It's your turn.	Ripeti.

PISTOL
(to Ford)

Then in a nutshell:	In due parole:
The monstrous Falstaff's planning	L'enorme Falstaff vuole
A raid upon your dwelling.	Entrar nel vostro tetto,
He means to steal your treasure	Beccarvi la consorte,
To pay for all his pleasure,	Sfondar la cassa-forte
And . . . to seduce your wife, sir!	E . . .sconquassarvi il letto.

DR CAIUS

Infamous!	Caspita!

FORD

Gods above!	Quanti guai!

BARDOLPH
(to Ford)

Billets-doux he has sent her . . .	Già le scrisse un biglietto . . .

PISTOL
(interrupting)

When asked to bear such vileness	Ma quel messaggio abbietto
I refused.	Ricusai.

BARDOLPH

I refused.	Ricusai.

PISTOL

Beware that man!	Badate a voi!

BARDOLPH

Beware him!	Badate!

73

PISTOL

If once you should let him in	Falstaff le occhieggia tutte,
He'll ogle all the women,	Che siano belle o brutte,
Young maidens, married women.	Pulzelle o maritate.

BARDOLPH

Maidens! Married women!	Tutte! Tutte! Tutte!
The adornments Diana once	La corona che adorna
Bestowed on Actaeon	D'Atteòn l'irte chiome
Will soon be yours, sir!	Su voi già spunta!

FORD

What	Come
Do you mean by that?	Sarebbe a dir?

BARDOLPH

The horns, Sir.	Le corna.

FORD

Ugly expression!	Brutta parola!

DR CAIUS

His amorous greed	Ha voglie
Matches his bulk.	Voraci il Cavaliere.

FORD

I'll keep a watch on Alice,	Sorveglierò la moglie.
I'll keep a watch on Falstaff,	Sorveglierò il messere.
(*The four women re-enter from the left.*)	
Protect whatever's mine,	Salvar vo'i beni miei
And guard it from his greed.	Dagli appetiti altrui.

FENTON
(*seeing Nannetta*)

(It's she.)	(È lei.)

NANETTA
(*seeing Fenton*)

(It's he.)	(È lui.)

FORD
(*seeing Alice*)

(It's she.)	(È lei.)

ALICE
(*seeing Ford*)

(It's he.)	(È lui.)

DR CAIUS
(*to Ford, indicating Alice*)

(It's she.)	(È lei.)

MEG
(*to Alice, indicating Ford*)

(It's he.)	(È lui.)

MEG
(*to the other women, indicating Ford, in a low voice*)

(If he suspected! . . .	(S'egli sapesse! . . .

NANNETTA

Careful!   Guai!

ALICE

Take care he doesn't meet us.	Schiviamo i passi suoi.

MEG

Is Ford so jealous?	Ford è geloso?

74

ALICE

Insanely.   Assai.

QUICKLY

Quiet.   Zitto.

ALICE

We'd better leave.)   Badiamo a noi.)

(*Alice, Meg and Quickly exeunt at left, leaving Nannetta. Ford, Dr Caius, Bardolph and Pistol exeunt at right, leaving Fenton.*)

FENTON
(*among the shrubs, to Nannetta, in a low voice*)

Pst, pst, Nannetta.   Pst, pst, Nannetta.

NANNETTA
(*putting her finger to her lips*)

Ssssh.   Ssss.

FENTON

Come here.   Vien qua.

NANNETTA

Quiet.   Taci.
What now?   Che vuoi?

FENTON

Two kisses.   Due baci.

NANNETTA

Then hurry.   In fretta.

FENTON

I'll hurry.   In fretta.
(*They kiss quickly, by the clump of trees.*)

NANNETTA

Lips that are burning!   [10]   Labbra di foco!

FENTON

Kisses that charm me!   Labbra di fiore! ...

NANNETTA

Lips that are learning   Che il vago gioco
Love will not harm me.   Sanno d'amore.

FENTON

Pearls gently shining,   Che spargon ciarle,
Now you reveal them,   Che mostran perle,
Sweet to behold them,   Belle a vederle,
Sweeter to conceal them!   Dolci a baciarle!
(*He tries to embrace her.*)
Lips that delight me!   Labbra leggiadre!

NANNETTA
(*defending herself and looking round anxiously*)

Hands taking chances!   Man malandrine!

FENTON

Eyes that invite me!   Ciglia assassine!
With fiery glances!   Pupille ladre!
I love you!   T'amo!
(*Fenton tries to kiss her again.*)

NANNETTA

But be careful.
No.

Imprudente.
No.

FENTON

Yes . . . Two kisses.

Sì . . . Due baci.

NANNETTA
(*frees herself*)

Careful.

Basta.

FENTON

Ah, how I
Love you!

Mi piaci
Tanto!

NANNETTA

They're coming.

Vien gente.

(*They separate as the women re-enter.*)

FENTON
(*singing as he hides himself among the trees upstage, not taking his eyes off Nannetta*)

"Bocca baciata non perde ventura." [11]

"Bocca baciata non perde ventura."

NANNETTA
(*continuing Fenton's song as she prepares to rejoin the women*)

"Anzi rinnova come fa la luna."

"Anzi rinnova come fa la luna."

ALICE

Falstaff has dared to slight me.

Falstaff m'ha canzonata.

MEG

He must be taught a lesson.

Merita un gran castigo.

ALICE

What if I wrote a letter?

Se gli scrivessi un rigo? . . .

NANNETTA
(*rejoining the group, as though nothing had happened*)

A messenger might be better.

Val meglio un'ambasciata.

ALICE

Yes.

Sì.

NANNETTA

Yes.

Sì.

QUICKLY

Yes.

Sì.

ALICE
(*to Quickly*)

So to the mountain
You'll go. And you must offer him
A tender encounter
With me.

Da quel brigante
Tu andrai. Lo adeschi all'offa
D'un ritrovo galante
Con me.

QUICKLY

Excellent notion!

Questa è gaglioffa!

NANNETTA

Cunning as ever!

Che bella burla!

ALICE

First
To attract our prey to us

Prima,
Per attirarlo a noi,

76

We must be charming . . .   Lo lusinghiamo . . .

NANNETTA

And then?   E poi?

ALICE

And then   . . . E poi
We'll teach him better manners.   Gliele cantiamo in rima.

QUICKLY

And then we'll let him have it.   Non merita riguardo.

ALICE

A monster.   È un bove.

MEG

A suitor who's   È un uomo senza
Deceitful.   Fede.

ALICE

A mountain of blubber.   È un monte di lardo.

MEG

In vain he'll beg for mercy.   Non merita clemenza.

ALICE

Bloated beast who must squander   È un ghiotton che scialacqua
All that he has on feeding.   Tutto il suo aver nel cuoco.

NANNETTA

We'll dump him in the river.   Lo tufferem nell'acqua.

ALICE

We'll roast him in the oven.   Lo arrostiremo al fuoco.

NANNETTA

Delightful!   Che gioia!

ALICE

We'll be merry!   Che allegria!

ALL

Delightful! Delightful!   Che gioia! Che gioia!

MEG
(*to Quickly*)

We count on you to play   Procaccia di far bene
Your part discreetly.   La tua parte.

QUICKLY
(*noticing Fenton who has made a movement in the shrubbery*)

Who's watching?   Chi viene?

MEG

I see there's someone spying.   Là c'è qualcun che spia.
(*Alice, Meg and Quickly exeunt rapidly at right. Nannetta remains and Fenton joins her.*)

FENTON

Back to the challenge.   Torno all'assalto.

NANNETTA
(*as if challenging Fenton*)

I must defy you.   Torno alla gara.
On guard, sir!   Ferisci!

77

Stop me!   Para!

*(He tries to kiss her. Nannetta covers her face with a hand which Fenton kisses and tries to kiss
again; but Nannetta lifts it as high as she can and Fenton tries in vain to reach it with his lips.)*

NANNETTA

You aim too high, sir.   La mira è in alto.
And love reverses rules   L'amor è un agile
Of warfare: it is his law   Torneo, sua corte
That the weaker sex   Vuol che il più fragile
Conquers the stronger.   Vinca il più forte.

FENTON

Love is an archer   M'armo, e ti guardo.
Who never misses.   T'aspetto al varco.

NANNETTA

Lips form his bowstring.   Il labbro è l'arco.

FENTON

His shafts are kisses.   E il bacio è il dardo.
Careful! A shaft   Bada! la freccia
From my bow will strike you,   Fatal già scocca
Launched by that archer,   Dalla mia bocca
Aimed at your tresses.   Sulla tua treccia.

(He kisses her hair.)

NANNETTA
(winding her hair about his neck while he kisses it)

Now you're my prisoner.   Eccoti avvinto.

FENTON

Captive for ever!   Chiedo la vita!

NANNETTA

I have been wounded,   Io son ferita,
You have been conquered.   Ma tu sei vinto.

FENTON

Be kind! Your prisoner   Pietà! Facciamo
Surrenders, and then . . .   La pace e poi . . .

NANNETTA

And then?   E poi?

FENTON

Why then,   Se vuoi,
On with the battle!   Ricominciamo.

NANNETTA

Peace is declared now,   Bello è quel gioco
Our duel is over.   Che dura poco.
Later.   Basta.

FENTON

How I love you!   Amor mio!

NANNETTA

They're coming. I leave you!   Vien gente. Addio!
(She runs off to the right.)

FENTON
(moving away, singing)

"Bocca baciata non perde ventura..."   "Bocca baciata non perde ventura..."

"Anzi rinnova come fa la luna."   "Anzi rinnova come fa la luna."

(*Ford, Dr Caius, Bardolph and Pistol re-enter; Fenton then joins them.*)

BARDOLPH
(*to Ford*)

To his long-winded speeches   Udrai quanta egli sfoggia
I've often been a martyr.   Magniloquenza altera.

FORD

You told me he was staying . . .   Dicesta ch'egli alloggia
Where?   Dove?

PISTOL

Staying at the Garter.   Alla Giarrettiera.

FORD

And there you will announce me,   A lui mi annuncerete,
But "Master Brook" you'll call me,   Ma con un falso nome;
And then we'll see if Falstaff   Poscia vedrete come
Accepts the bait I offer.   Lo piglio nella rete.
But you must keep my secret.   Ma . . . non una parola.

BARDOLPH

I'm not a man to chatter.   In ciarle non m'ingolfo.
My name is Bardolph.   Io mi chiamo Bardolfo.

PISTOL

And my name is Pistol.   Io mi chiamo Pistola.

FORD

We're agreed?   Siam d'accordo.

BARDOLPH

          Your secret's   L'arcano
Safe with me.   Custodirem.

PISTOL

          And I'll not   Son sordo
Breathe a word.   E muto.

FORD

          And so we're all   Siam d'accordo
Agreed.   Tutti.

BARDOLPH *and* **PISTOL**

     Yes.   Si.

FORD

     Here's my hand.   Qua la mano.

(*Enter Alice, Nannetta, Meg and Quickly upstage.*)

(Alice, Nannetta, Meg, and Mistress Quickly come on at the back, while the five men embark on the verses below. Their quintet soon becomes a nonet as the four women repeat, in part, their ensemble on page 71. Fenton's voice, supported by the orchestral horns, soars in an independent line.)

DR CAIUS
(to Ford)

For your barbarous predicament	Del tuo barbaro diagnostico
I've a cure that is infallible.	Forse il male è assai men barbaro.
To confession you must urge him,	Ti convien tentar la prova
I will tell you what to do.	Molestissima del ver.
Go to work like a medicament	Così avvien col zapor ostico
Made of rhubarb or of calomel,	Del ginepro e del rabarbaro;
Of his secrets you must purge him	Il benessere rinnova
And discover what is true.	L'amarissimo bicchier.

PISTOL
(to Ford)

You must soak the man with sherry,	Voi dovete empirgli il calice.
You must fill his bumper steadily;	Tratto tratto, interrogandolo,
When Sir John is truly merry,	Per tantar se vi riesca
He will tell his secrets readily.	Di trover del nodo il bandolo.
As the willow bends to water,	Come all'acqua inclina il salice
So John Falstaff bends to wine,	Così al vin quel Cavalier.
And his plan you will discover,	Scoverete la sua tresca
All his secrets you'll divine.	Scoprirete il suo pensier.

FORD
(to Pistol)

I shall trap that lustful elephant,	Tu vedrai sa bene adopera
That obese inflated fellow;	L'arte mia con quell'infame.
He's an ox who thinks he's elegant,	E sarà prezzo dell'opera
When I catch him he will bellow.	S'io discopro le sue trame.
For I mean to make him penitent	Se de ma storno il ridicolo
That he tried to woo my wife.	Non avrem oprato invan,
When I catch him I shall beat him,	Se l'attiro nel'inganno
He'll regret it all his life.	L'angue morde il cerretan.

BARDOLPH
(to Ford)

Master Ford, a crisis threatens	Messer Ford, un infortunio
And you face a great calamity.	Marital in voi s'incorpora:
If you're not astute and cautious	Se non siete astuto e cauto
By Sir John you'll be betrayed.	Quel Sir John vi tradirà.
For that purple-blooded pumpkin	Quel paffuto plenilunio
Is a seething mass of vanity,	Che il color del vino imporpora
And his plan to win your lady	Troverebbe un pasto lauto
Has been well and truly laid.	Nella vostra ingenuità.

FENTON
(to himself)

Here a group of men is muttering,	Qua borbotta un crocchio d'uomini.
And I fear there's mischief brewing.	C'è nell'aria una malìa.
There's a flock of women chattering,	Là cinguette un stuol di femine,
They are planning something too.	Spira un vento agitator.
Ah, my loved one, my heart is yours alone.	Ma colei che in cor mi nomini,
Ah, my love, no power can part us.	Dolce amor, vuol esser mia!
We shall live like two twin stars	Noi sarem come due gemine
Shining brightly, whom love unites as one.	Stelle unite in un ardor.

(Exeunt Ford, Dr Caius, Fenton, Bardolph and Pistol.)

	ALICE
Enough of this chattering.	Qui più non si vagoli . . .

NANNETTA
(to Quickly)

So off to attract	Tu corri all'ufficio
Our prey.	Tuo.

ALICE

Soon he'll be miaowing	Vo'ch'egli miagoli
With love like a tom-cat.	D'amor come un micio.

(to Quickly)

You'll trick him.	E intesa.

QUICKLY

Yes.	Sì.

NANNETTA

It's settled.	È detta.

ALICE

Tomorrow.	Domani.

QUICKLY

Yes. Yes.	Sì. Sì.

ALICE

Goodbye, Meg.	Buon dì, Meg.

QUICKLY

Nannetta,	Nannetta.
Goodbye.	Buon dí.

NANNETTA

Goodbye.	Addio.

MEG

Goodbye.	Buon dì.

ALICE
(keeping the others back a moment)

You'll see how his belly	Vedrai che quell'epa
Grows larger and larger	Terribile e tronfia
Expanding . . .	Si gonfia . . .

ALICE *and* **NANNETTA**

Expanding . . .	Si gonfia . . .

ALICE, MEG, QUICKLY, NANNETTA

Expanding until it bursts!	Si gonfia e poi crepa.

ALICE

"My radiant glances will shine on him with love . . . "	"Ma il viso mio su lui risplenderà . . ."

ALL

"Shine like the starlight, like a shining star in heaven above."	"Come una stella sull'immensità."

(They break into laughter as they take leave of one another and go.)

Act Two

Part One. *Inside the Garter Inn. As in Act One, Part One.* **Falstaff** *is stretched out in his big chair in his usual position, drinking his sherry sack.* **Bardolph** *and* **Pistol** *are near the door at the left. Later,* **Mistress Quickly.**

BARDOLPH, PISTOL
(singing in unison and beating their breasts in an act of contrition)

We're repentant, conscience smites us. | Siam pentiti e contriti.

FALSTAFF
(barely turning to them)

Villains return to vice, | L'uomo ritorna al vizio,
Like mice to the larder . . . | La gatta al lardo . . .

BARDOLPH, PISTOL

And we return again to serve you. | E noi, torniamo al tuo servizio.

BARDOLPH
(to Falstaff)

Sir John, here at the door a certain lady is waiting, | Padron, là c'è una donna che alla vostra presenza
Hoping you will receive her. | Chiede d'essere ammessa.

FALSTAFF

Admit her. | S'inoltri.

(Exit Bardolph left, returning immediately with Mistress Quickly.)

QUICKLY
(dropping a deep curtsey to Falstaff, who remains seated)

O Your Worship! [12] | Reverenza!

FALSTAFF

Good day, my worthy woman. | Buon giorno, buona donna.

QUICKLY

O Your Worship! And if you will allow me, | Reverenza! Se Vostra Grazia vuole,
(approaching him with great respect and caution)
I'd like a word in private; secrets I have to tell you. | Vorrei, segretamente, dirle quattro parole.

FALSTAFF

I grant you audience. | T'accordo udienza.
(to Bardolph and Pistol, who have remained at the back to spy)
Be off now. | Escite.
(They go out left, pulling faces.)

QUICKLY

O Your Worship! I come from | Reverenza! Madonna
(softly)
Mistress Ford. | Alice Ford . . .

FALSTAFF
(rising and moving eagerly towards her)

Speak on! | Ebben?

QUICKLY

Ah me! Unhappy lady! [13] | Ahimè! Povera donna!
You're a wicked seducer! | Siete un gran seduttore!

FALSTAFF
(promptly)

I know. Continue. | Lo so. Continua.

QUICKLY

Good Alice | Alice
Is trembling with unquenchable love for you; she says | Sta in grande agitazione d'amor per voi; vi dice

Your letter has brought such joy to her, asks me to thank you,
And to say her husband is absent from two [14] till three.

Ch'ebbe la vostra lettera, che vi ringrazia e che
Suo marito esce sempre dalle due alle tre.

FALSTAFF

From two till three.

Dalle due alle tre.

QUICKLY

And Your Worship in that hour
May freely come to greet her and bring some consolation
To lovely Alice. Unhappy lady! For day and night
She suffers cruelly! From a husband who's jealous!

Vostra Grazia a quell'ora
Potrà liberamente salir ove dimora
La bella Alice. Povera donna! le angosce sue
Son crudeli! ha un marito geloso!

FALSTAFF
(reflecting on Quickly's words)

From two   Dalle due
Till three.   Alle tre.

(to Quickly)

Tell your mistress I await the hour
With impatience. When love commands, I must obey.

Le dirai che impaziente aspetto
Quell'ora. Al mio dovere non mancherò.

QUICKLY

God bless you.   Ben detto.
But that's not all the news that I bring Your Worship.

Ma c'è un altra ambasciata per Vostra Grazia.

FALSTAFF

Speak on.   Parla.

QUICKLY

The lovely Meg (inspiring love in everyone who sees her)
Has also bade me bring you loving and tender greeting;
But she regrets her husband is very seldom absent
Unhappy lady! As pure as snow is that innocent heart!
You are a great magician.

La bella Meg (un angelo che innamora a guardarla)
Anch'essa vi saluta molto amorosamente;
Dice che suo marito è assai di rado assente.
Povera donna! un giglio di candore e di fè!
Voi le stregate tutte.

FALSTAFF

I use no magic art,   Stregoneria non c'è.
But merely wield a certain charm of my own ... One thing ...
They'll not tell one another?

Ma un certo qual mio fascino personal! ...
Dimmi: L'altra sa di quest'altra?

QUICKLY

Oh no! We women keep our secrets.   Oibò! La donna nasce scaltra.
You can trust us.   Non temete.

FALSTAFF
(searching in his purse)

You deserve a fine reward ...   Or ti vo' remunerar ...

QUICKLY

Who sows generous   Chi semina
Favours, will harvest love.   Grazie, raccoglie amore.

FALSTAFF
(taking out a coin and handing it to Quickly)

Take this, Mercurial messenger.   Prendi, Mercurio-femina.
(dismissing her with a gesture)
Be sure to greet both ladies.   Saluta le due dame.

Your Worship.   M'inchino.

(*Exit.*)

Falstaff *remains alone. Then enter* **Bardolph**, *then* **Ford**, *then* **Pistol**.

FALSTAFF

I've won my Alice! [15]   Alice è mia!
Jack, go your ways. Go, go, glory awaits you.   Va, vecchio John, va, va per la tua via.
This old capacious body is still preparing   Questa tua vecchia carne ancora spreme
New kinds of joy for you.   Qualche dolcezza a te.
Beautiful ladies still defy their husbands   Tutte le donne ammutinate insieme
To damn themselves for me!   Si dannano per me!
Good paunch of old Sir John, I've fed you   Buon corpo di Sir John, ch'io nutro e
  royally,   sazio,
Now you reward me.   Va, ti ringrazio.

BARDOLPH
(*entering from the left*)

Sir John, outside, there is a certain Master   Padron, di là c'è un certo Mastro Fontana
Brook who is most eager to exchange a   che anela di conoscervi;
word with you;
He offers you a demijohn of Cyprus wine,   Offre una damigiana di Cipro per l'asciolvere
and wishes you a pleasant morning.   di Vostra Signoria.

FALSTAFF

Master Brook did you call him?   Il suo nome è Fontana?

BARDOLPH

Yes.   Sì.

FALSTAFF

Welcome brook   Benne accolta sia
That flows with wine of Cyprus, and   La fontana che spande un simile liquore!
overflows in such abundance!
Admit him.   Entri.
(*Exit Bardolph.*)
Jack, go your ways, glory awaits you!   Va, vecchio John, per la tua via.

(*Ford in disguise enters left, preceded by Bardolph, who pauses at the door and bows as he goes
past, and followed by Pistol carrying a demijohn which he puts on the table. Pistol and Bardolph
remain in the background. Ford has a small sack in his hand.*)

FORD
(*coming forward, after bowing deeply to Falstaff*)

Sir John,
May heaven protect you!   Signore,
                                 V'asista il cielo!

FALSTAFF
(*returning the greeting*)

May heaven, sir, protect you also.   Assista voi pur, signore.

FORD

(*still obsequious*)

I am,   Io sono,
I admit, unceremonious but I hope you'll   Davver, molto indiscreto, e vi chiedo
forgive me   perdono,
If it was disrespectful to venture to   Se, senza cerimonie, qui vengo e
approach you   sprovveduto
In this highly informal way.   Di più lunghi preamboli.

FALSTAFF

You could not be more welcome.   Voi siete il benvenuto.

FORD

In me you see a man who's blessed with   In me vedete un uomo ch'ha un'abbondanza
great abundance,   grande
A man of wealth and substance, a man   Degli agi della vita; un uom che spende
prepared to spend   e spande

And never ask what it costs me, when
something takes my fancy.
Master Brook stands before you!

Come più gli talenta pur di passar
mattana.
Io mi chiamo Fontana!

FALSTAFF
(advancing to shake his hand with great cordiality)

Dear Master Brook, I greet you! [16]
From the moment we met you made a fine
impression.

Caro signor Fontana!
Voglio fare con voi più ampia conoscenza.

FORD

Dearest Sir John, I would like a word or
two with you in private.

Caro Sir John, desidero parlarvi in
confidenza.

BARDOLPH
(to Pistol, watching from behind)

(Attention!

(Attento!

PISTOL
(to Bardolph)

Quiet!

Zitto!

BARDOLPH

Watch him! He's rising! Ford's
hook is baited,
Gold will attract him.

Guarda. Scommetto! Egli va
dritto
Nel trabocchetto.

PISTOL

Falstaff will swallow it . . .

Ford se lo intrappola . . .

BARDOLPH, PISTOL

Quiet!)

Zitto!)

FALSTAFF
(to Bardolph and Pistol, who leave at a sign from him)

You two begone!

Che fate là?
(to Ford, with whom he remains alone)

I'm listening.

V'ascolto.

FORD

Sir John, I am emboldened
To recall what the well known proverb
says: with a key
Made of gold all doors can be opened, for
gold's a mighty talisman,
And gold can conquer all things.

Sir John, m'infonde ardire
Un ben noto proverbio popolar: si suol dire
Che l'oro apre ogni porta, che l'oro è un
talismano,
Che l'oro vince tutto.

FALSTAFF

Gold's an excellent captain,
Who leads to victory.

L'oro è un buon capitano
Che marcia avanti.

FORD
(approaching the table)

Exactly. And I've a bag of money here
Weighing far too much. Sir John, I'd like to
ask
If you would share my burden . . .

Ebbene. Ho un sacco di monete
Qua, che mi pesa assai. Sir John, se voi
volete
Aiutarmi a portarlo . . .

FALSTAFF
(He takes the sack and puts it on the table.)

I shan't refuse . . . but why, I pray:
I have done nothing to deserve it . . .

Con gran piacer . . . non so,
Davver, per qual mio merito, Messere . . .

FORD

Let me explain.
In Windsor there's a lady, lovely and bright [17]
and charming;
Her name is Alice; she's married to a
certain Ford.

Ve lo dirò.
C'è a Windsor una dama, bella e leggiadra
molto.
Si chiama Alice; è moglie d'un certo Ford.

FALSTAFF

Continue.

V'ascolto.

FORD

I love her; she does not love me. I write her; she won't answer.
Observe her; she hides her glances. I seek her; and cannot find her.
On her I spent my fortune, a thousand gifts[18] I gave her,
With trembling heart I wooed her, and tried to win her favour.
Ah me! All this was useless! And standing on her doorstep,
Rejected, and empty-handed, I sang this madrigal . . .

Io l'amo e lei non m'ama; le scrivo, non risponde;
La guardo, non mi guarda; la cerco e si nasconde.
Per lei sprecai tesori, gittai doni su doni,
Escogitai, tremando, il vol delle occasioni.
Ahimè! tutto fu vano! Rimasi sulle scale,
Negletto, a bocca asciutta, cantando . . . un madrigale.

FALSTAFF
(*carolling merrily*)

"Ah love! Ah Love! All men alive acclaim you,
But cannot ever tame you."

"L'amor, l'amor che non ci dà mai tregue
Finché la vita strugge . . ."

FORD
(*joining in the cadence*)

" . . . tame you!"

" . . . strugge."

FALSTAFF

"And like a shadow . . ."

"E come l'ombra . . ."

FORD

" . . . when you fly us . . ."

". . . che chi fugge . . ."

FALSTAFF

". . . we follow . . ."

" . . . insegue . . ."

FORD

"But when we follow . . ."

"E chi l'insegue . . ."

FALSTAFF

" . . . fly us . . ."

" . . . fugge . . ."

FORD

All men this truth discover; I learned it to my cost.

E questo madrigale l'ho appreso a prezzo d'ôr.

FALSTAFF

There speaks a hapless lover, a man who loved and lost.

Quest'è il destin fatale del misero amator.

FORD

"Ah love! Ah love! All men alive acclaim you . . ."

"L'amor, l'amor che non ci da mai tregue . . ."

FALSTAFF

And she never once encouraged your wooing?

Essa non vi die' mai luogo a lusinghe?

FORD

No.

No.

FALSTAFF

But say; why tell your tale to me?

Ma infin, perché v'aprite a me?

FORD

Let me explain:
You are a man of breeding, prowess, persuasion, compassion,
You are a man of valour, a man of fame and fashion . . .

Ve lo dirò:
Voi siete un gentiluomo prode, arguto, facondo,
Voi siete un uom di guerra, voi siete un uom di mondo . . .

FALSTAFF
(*with a deprecatory gesture*)

Oh! . . .

Oh! . . .

I don't flatter, so take this bag of gold and spend it,	Non vi adulo, e quello è un sacco di monete:
Yes, spend it all! Spend it all! When it's done, spend and squander	Spendetele! spendetele! si, spendete e spandete
All the gold that I'm possessed of! And be prosperous and happy!	Tutto il mio patrimonio! Siate ricco e felice!
But, in exchange then, conquer the heart of my fair Alice Ford!	Ma, in contraccambio, chiedo che conquistiate Alice!

FALSTAFF

Curious request!	Strana ingiunzion!

FORD

It's simple: though I may woo in vain, [19]	Mi spiego: quella crudel beltà
I know that all her coldness springs from her sense of pride.	Sempre è vissuta in grande fede di castità.
She deems it is her duty to make a show of virtue,	La sua virtù importuna m'abbarbagliava gli occhi:
Her cold and cruel beauty seems to say: "Don't dare to touch me!"	La bella inespugnabile dicea: "Guai se me tocchi."
But if you once should win her, then I could win her too;	Ma se voi l'espugnate, poi, posso anch' io sperar:
For one fall means a new fall, and so . . . What do you say?	Da fallo nasce fallo e allor . . . Che ve ne par?

FALSTAFF

What do I say? I have my answer ready, so first	Prima di tutto, senza complimenti, Messere,
I'll take your money. Then – yes, by my knightly honour;	Accetto il sacco. E poi (fede di cavaliere,
You may trust me! – I'll satisfy your ardent yearning.	Qua la mano!) farò le vostre brame sazie.

(shaking Ford's hand warmly)

You shall have Mistress Ford for your enjoyment.	Voi, la moglie di Ford possederete.

FORD

Thank you!	Grazie!

FORD

To me she shows much favour; (I see no cause to hide it	Io son già molto innannzi; (non c'è ragion ch'io taccia
From you) in half an hour she'll be in my embraces.	Con voi) fra una mezz'ora sarà nelle mie braccia.

FORD

Who?	Chi?

FALSTAFF

Your Alice. Not long ago her faithful handmaid came in secret	Alice. Essa mandò dianzi una . . . confidente
To tell me that that simpleton who is her husband is absent	Per dirmi che quel tanghero di suo marito è assente
From two till three.	Dalle due alle tre.

FORD

But do you know him?	Lo conoscete?

FALSTAFF

Not I! I hope	Il diavolo
That the devil will claim him, like Menelaus his ancestor!	Se lo porti all'inferno con Menelao suo avolo!
You'll see! I'll horn the buffalo, willy-nilly! [20] If he oppose me	Vedrai! Te lo cornifico netto! se mi frastorna
I'll bash those branching horns of his until he cries for mercy!	Gli sparo una girandola di botte sulle corna!
Silly old Ford's a jackass! A jackass! He'll be a cuckold,	Quel Messer Ford e un bue! Un bue! Te lo corbello,

You'll see! Time's passing. So wait for me here. I must shine in splendour.

Vedrai! Ma è tardi. Aspettami qua. Vado a farmi bello.

(He takes the sack of money and goes out at the back.)

FORD *alone, then* FALSTAFF

FORD

I'm dreaming? Or is this true ... I feel two monstrous
Horns that grow from my forehead!
Am I dreaming? Master Ford! Master Ford! Dreaming?
Rouse yourself! Up! To action!
Your wife betrays you, betrays your reputation
And your name, and your honour, and her virtue!
Planned to the minute! Prepared to betray you!
You are mocked and derided!
They dare to tell us [21]
That a sensible husband's never jealous!

Behind my back I seem to hear my neighbours
Laugh when they see me murmuring and jeering.

O holy wedlock, I curse you!
Woman, I curse you!
Who but a fool puts his faith in a woman!

I could entrust
All my beer to a German,
All of my larder
To a greedy Dutchman,
Entrust my whisky to an Irish toper —
Not my wife with my honour! O cruel misfortune!

And that hideous word again torments me:
A cuckold! Jackass! Buffoon! Blockhead!
Fool of a husband!
Ah! *A cuckold! A cuckold!*

But you will not escape! No! Filthy, guilty,
Accursed lascivious lecher!

First let him meet her,
And then I'll catch them! I'm choking!
I shall avenge this outrage!

O jealous heart, I thank you,
My eyes are blind no more! You'll not deceive me!

È sogno? o realtà ... Due rami enormi
Crescon sulla mia testa.
È un sogno? Mastro Ford! Mastro Ford! Dormi?
Svegliati! Su! ti desta!
Tua moglie sgarra e mette in mal assetto
L'onor tuo, la tua casa ed il tuo letto!
L'ora è fissata, tramato l'inganno;
Sei gabbato e truffato! ...
E poi diranno
Che un marito geloso è un insensato!

Già dietro a me nomi d'infame conio
Fischian passando; mormora lo scherno.

O matrimonio: Inferno!
Donna: demonio!
Nella lor moglie abbian fede i babbei!

Affiderei
La mia birra a un Tedesco,
Tutto il mio desco,
A un Olandese lurco,
La mia bottiglia d'acquavite a un Turco,
Non mia moglie a se stessa. O laida sorte!

Quella brutta parola in cor mi torna:
Le corna! Bue! Capron! le fusa torte!
Ah! *le corna! le corna!*

Ma non mu sfuggirai! no! sozzo, reo,
Dannato epicureo!

Prima li accoppio
E poi li colgo. Io scoppio!
Vendicherò l'affronto!

[22] Laudata sempre sia
Nel fondo del mio cor la gelosia.

FALSTAFF
(re-entering upstage centre. He wears a new doublet and has a hat and cane.) [23]

Look at me now! I'm ready.
Shall we set forth together?

Eccomi qua. Son pronto.
M'accompagnate un tratto?

FORD

I'll start you on your journey.

Vi metto sulla via.

(They start off. As they reach the door each makes polite signs to the other to precede him.)

FALSTAFF

You go first.

Prima voi.

FORD

You go first.

Prima voi.

FALSTAFF

No. This is my poor dwelling.

No, sono in casa mia.

88

(drawing back a little)

Precede me.	Passate.

FORD

You first ...	Prego ...

FALSTAFF

Time's passing. The rendez-vous is pressing.	È tardi. L'appuntamento preme.

FORD

So lead the way, I beg you ...	Non fate complimenti ...

FALSTAFF

Ah, well we'll leave together.	Ebben; passiamo insieme.

(Falstaff tucks Ford's arm under his, and they go out arm-in-arm.)

Part Two. *A large room in Ford's house. A broad window at the back. A door on the right, a door on the left, and another door near the right-hand corner, leading to the staircase. Another staircase in the left-hand corner. Through the big window, which is wide open, the garden is seen. A closed screen is leaning against the left-hand wall, next to a huge fireplace. A wardrobe is set against the right wall. A little table, a chest-seat. Against the walls, an armchair and some seats. On the armchair, a lute. Flowers on the table.*
Alice, Meg, *then, from the right-hand door,* **Mistress Quickly,** *laughing. Then* **Nannetta.**

ALICE

We'll send a bill to Parliament demanding Heavy taxes on men as fat as Falstaff.	Presenteremo un *bill*, per una tassa Al parlamento, sulla gente grassa.

QUICKLY
(entering)

Good ladies!	Comari!

ALICE
(hurrying towards Quickly with Meg, while Nannetta, entering at the same time, stands sadly apart)

What now?	Ebben?

MEG

What news?	Che c'è?

QUICKLY

Our plan is working!	Sarà sconfitto!

ALICE

Well done!	Brava!

QUICKLY

And soon we shall have snared the monster!	Fra poco gli farem la festa!

ALICE, MEG

Perfect!	Bene!

QUICKLY

He tumbled headlong into my pitfall.	Piombò nel laccio a capofitto.

ALICE

Do tell us how it happened.	Narrami tutto, lesta.

MEG

Tell us.	Lesta.

ALICE

Tell us.	Lesta.

QUICKLY

I sally forth until I reach the Garter, And I ask to be taken to the presence Of the knight, to give a secret message.	[24] Giunta all'Albergo della Giarrettiera Chiedo d'essere ammessa alla presenza Del Cavalier, segreta messaggera.

Sir John is gracious, and he grants me audience,
And he receives me with pompous con-descension:
"Good day, my worthy woman."
"O Your Worship!"
I drop a curtsey, bending very low be-
Fore him; my confidential message follows.
Each word he savours, and every morsel that I
Offer him, he swallows.
So he, to put it briefly, [25]
Believes you two ladies are fired by frenzied longing,
And ardently adore him.

Sir John si degna d'accordarmi udienza,
M'accoglie tronfio in furfantesca posa:
"Buon giorno, buona donna."
"Reverenza."
A lui m'inchino molto ossequiosa-
Mente, poi passo alle notizie ghiotte.
Lui beve grosso ed ogni mia massiccia
Frottola inghiotte.
Infin, per farla spiccia,
Vi crede entrambe innamorate cotte
Delle bellezze sue.

(to Alice)
And soon you'll see him falling at your feet.

E lo vedrete presto ai vostri piè.

ALICE

How soon?

Quando?

QUICKLY

Shortly. Here. From two till three.

Oggi, qui, dalle due alle tre.

MEG

From two till three!

Dalle due alle tre.

ALICE
(looking at the clock)

It's two already.

Son già le due.

(running to the door upstage and calling)
Come here, Ned! Will!

Olà! Ned! Will!

(to Quickly) [26]
I've made my plan already.

Già tutto ho preparato.

(She goes back to call out to the people in the garden again.)
Bring in that basket filled with dirty laundry!

Portate qui la cesta del bucato.

QUICKLY

A merry trick we'll play him!

Sarà un affare guaio!

ALICE

Nannetta, why aren't you laughing? What is wrong?

Nannetta, e tu non ridi? Che cos'hai?

(going to Nannetta and carressing her)
You're crying? What is wrong? Come tell your mother.

Tu piangi? Che cos'hai? Dillo a tua madre.

NANNETTA
(sobbing)

My father ...

Mio padre ...

ALICE

Go on ...

Ebben?

NANNETTA

My father ...

Mio padre ...

ALICE

Go on ...

Ebben?

NANNETTA

My father ...

Mio padre ...

(bursting into tears)
Tells me that I must marry Doctor Caius!

Vuole ch'io mi mariti al Doctor Cajo!!

ALICE

That ancient Frenchman?!

A quel pedante?!

QUICKLY

Oh no!

Oibò!

MEG

He's a buzzard!   A quel gonzo!

ALICE

He's a dullard!   A quel grullo!

NANNETTA

A rattling bag of bones!   A quel bisavolo!

ALICE

No! No!   No! No!

MEG, QUICKLY

No! No!   No! No!

ALL

No! No!   No! No!

NANNETTA

I'll die before I will accept him . . .   Piuttosto lapidata viva . . .

ALICE

Better be buried alive than be wed to him.   Da una mitraglia di torsi di cavolo.

QUICKLY

No question!   Ben detto!

MEG

Surely!   Brava!

ALICE

Have no fear.   Non temer.

NANNETTA
(jumping for joy)

Thank heaven!   Evviva!
To Doctor Caius my reply is No!   Col Dottor Cajo non mi sposerò!
(Meanwhile two manservants enter carrying a basket full of laundry.)

ALICE
(to the servants)

Set it down there. Then, when I call you again,   Mettete là. Poi, quando avrò chiamato,
Take up the basket and empty it into the river.   Vuoterete la cesta nel fossato.

NANNETTA

Boom!   Bum!

ALICE
(to Nannetta)

Quiet!   Taci.
(to the servants)
That's all now.   Andate.
(The servants leave.)

NANNETTA

Riverside explosion!   Che bombardamento!

ALICE

Set the scene for his entry.   Prepariamo la scena.
(running to fetch a chair and placing it by the table)
Here, a chair.   Qua una sedia.

NANNETTA
(She hurries to take her lute and put it on the table.)

Here, my lute.   Qua il mio liuto.

ALICE

The screen a little open.   Apriamo il paravento.
(Nannetta and Meg run to fetch the screen, position it between the laundry-basket and the fireplace, and open it out.)

That's excellent! We're set. – A little wider.
The company is ready. Raise the curtain!
Merry wives of Windsor! The time is here!
Now we shall make the sky resound with
    our laughter!
Laughter that crackles and flashes and
    dances,
Explodes into fragments
That sparkle and glitter!
Merry companions! O wives of Windsor!
Sharpen your glances,
Glittering lances,
Mirth is the weapon when women rebel!
We'll show jealous husbands
That wives can be merry
Yet be true as well

Bravissime! Così. – Più aperto ancora.
Fra poco s'incomincia la commedia.
Gaie comari di Windsor! è l'ora!
L'ora d'alzar la risata sonora!

L'alta risata che scoppia, che scherza,
Che sfolgora, armata
Di dardi e di sferza!
Gaie comari, festosa brigata!
Sul lieto viso
Spunti il sorriso,
Splenda del riso – l'acuto fulgor!
Favilla incendiaria
Di gioia nell'aria
Di gioia nel cor.

(to Meg)

Prepare! You remember
Your role, when to enter?

A noi! – Tu la parte
Farai che ti spetta.

MEG
(to Alice)

You're sure there's no danger
That you might be crushed?

Tu corri il tuo rischio
Col grosso compar.

QUICKLY

I'll act as a sentry.

Io sto alla vedetta.

ALICE
(to Quickly)

Remember the signal.

Se sbagli ti fischio.

NANNETTA

I'll hide in the hallway
To see all is safe.

Io resto in disparte
Sull'uscio a spiar.

ALICE

And we shall show all men that harmless
    jokes
Played by honest women merely confirm
    their virtue.
It's the wicked ones, secretive and
    shameless,
Who seem to be most blameless.

E mostreremo all'uom che l'allegria

D'oneste donne ogni onestà comporta.

Fra le femine quella è la più ria

Che fa la gattamorta.

ALICE, NANNETTA, MEG

Merry wives of Windsor, be ready,
Be ready to laugh for soon the sky
Will be ringing and singing with laughter!

[27] Gaie comari di Windsor! è l'ora!
L'ora d'alzar la risata sonora!
(repeat)

QUICKLY
(who has gone to the window)

There he is! Outside!

Eccolo! È lui!

ALICE

How close?

Dov'è?

QUICKLY

Turning the corner.

Poco discosto.

NANNETTA

Hurry.

Presto.

QUICKLY

He's about to enter.

A salir s'avvia.

ALICE
(first to Nannetta, pointing to the left-hand door, then to Meg, pointing to the right-hand door)

You in there! You in there!

Tu di qua. Tu di là!

92

Positioned?   Al posto!

I'm ready!   Al posto!

QUICKLY
(*Exit, upstage centre.*)

I'm ready!   Al posto!

Alice *alone.* Then **Falstaff.** *Then* **Quickly.** *Then* **Meg.**

(*Alice seats herself at the table, takes the lute and touches a few chords.*)

FALSTAFF
(*He makes a sprightly entrance. Seeing Alice playing, he begins to warble.*)

"At last I pluck thee,   "Alfin t'ho colto,
My fragrant blossom,   Raggiante fior,
I pluck thee!"   T'ho colto!"

(*He takes Alice by the waist. She stops playing and rises.*)

Now when I die, I'll die contented.   Ed or potrò morir felice.
What more can life afford me   Avrò vissuto molto
Once I've enjoyed this blessed hour of   Dopo quest'ora di beato amor.
love?

ALICE

O enchanting Sir John!   O soave Sir John!

FALSTAFF

My lovely Alice!   Mia bella Alice!
I've no talent for compliments,   Non so far lo svenevole,
Flattering words, or fine flowery phrases,   Né lusingar, né usar frase fiorita,
But in plain English I'll express my wicked   Ma dirò tosto un mio pensier colpevole.
thought.

ALICE

What's that?   Coiè?

FALSTAFF

What's that: Coiè:
I wish that Master Ford   Vorrei che Mastro Ford
Was singing with the angels . . .   Passasse a miglior vita . . .

ALICE

But why?   Perché?

FALSTAFF

But why? You ask me?   Perché? Lo chiedi?
Then you would be my Lady   Saresti la mia Lady
With Falstaff as your Lord.   E Falstaff il tuo Lord.

ALICE

Poor sort of Lady, I!   Povera Lady inver!

FALSTAFF

Fit for a king.   Degna d'un Re.
I picture you adorned with my resplendent   T'immagino fregiata del mio stemma,
name,
Midst emeralds, pearls, and rubies   Mostrar fra gemma e gemma
Your lovely bosom gleams.   La pompa del tuo sen.
Those dazzling gems encircle you, their   Nell'iri ardente e mobile dei rai
blaze
Your charms revealing,   Dell'Adamante,
From gold-encrusted farthingale,   Col picchio pie' nel nobile
Two tiny feet come stealing,   Cerchio d'un guardinfante
And you will shine   Risplenderai
More gloriously than any rainbow ever seen.   Più fulgida d'un ampio arcobalen.

Those splendid gems I fear would blind me,
I have no taste for all you propose.
I tie this simple scarf behind me,
My sole adornment, an English rose.

Ogni più bel gioiel mi nuoce e spregio
Il finto idolo d'or.
Mi basta un vel legato in croce, un fregio
Al cinto e in testa un fior.

(She puts a flower in her hair.)

FALSTAFF
(about to embrace her)

Seductress!

Sirena!

ALICE
(taking a step backwards)

Flattering knight!

Adulator!

FALSTAFF

So we're alone
Where no one can disturb us.

Soli noi siamo
E non temiamo agguato.

ALICE

And so?

Ebben?

FALSTAFF

I love you!

Io t'amo!

ALICE
(moving away from him slightly)

A sinful thought inspires you!

Voi siete nel peccato!

FALSTAFF
(moving closer)

A man in love can't be accused of sinning.

Sempre l'amor l'occasione azzecca.

ALICE

Sir John!

Sir John!

FALSTAFF

The joys of love are just beginning.
I love you! Can you dare to blame me?

Chi segue vocazion non pecca.
T'amo! e non è mia colpa . . .

ALICE
(interrupting him playfully)

I fear your ample flesh is all too willing . . .

Se tanta avete vulnerabil polpa . . .

FALSTAFF

I was a page
To the merry Duke of York, tripped through
the maze of the dance like a fairy.
I was a vision
Slender, delightful, entrancing and airy –
yes airy!
Those were the days when I could cut a
caper,
Dance through the sunbeams, flitting like
a vapour,
I was a stripling, as spry as a sparrow,
Slipping through a thumb-ring as swift as
an arrow.

[28] Quand'ero paggio
Del Duca di Norfolk ero sottile, sottile,
sottile,
Ero un miraggio
Vago, leggero, gentile, gentile, gentile.

Quello era il tempo del mio verde Aprile,

Quello era il tempo del mio lieto Maggio,

Tant'ero smilzo, flessibile e snello
Che avrei guizzato attraverso un anello.

ALICE

You do but mock me.
I know that you deceive me.
I have a rival . . .

Voi mi celiate,
Io temo vostri inganni.
Temo che amiate . . .

FALSTAFF

Who?

Chi?

ALICE

Meg.

Meg.

FALSTAFF

Not her! I hate her ugly features.   Colei? M'è in uggia la sua faccia.

ALICE

Don't deceive me, my John ...   Non traditemi, John ...

FALSTAFF

A thousand years I   Mi par mill'anni
Have waited to embrace you.   D'averti fra le braccia.
(chasing her and trying to embrace her)
I love you ...   T'amo ...

ALICE
(defending herself)

For pity's sake!   Per carità ...

FALSTAFF
(seizing her by the waist)

Mine now!   Vieni!

QUICKLY
(shouting from the hall)

Good Mistress Alice!   Signora Alice!

FALSTAFF
(abandoning Alice, distressed)

Who is there?   Chi va là?

QUICKLY
(entering in pretended agitation)

Good Mistress Alice!   Signora Alice!

ALICE

Who's there?   Chi c'è?

QUICKLY
(tumbling over her words)

O my lady!   Mia signora!
It's Mistress Meg, she wants to see you, [29] C'è Mistress Meg e vuol parlarvi,
  huffing ...   sbuffa ...
Puffing, and panting ...   Strepita, s'abbaruffa ...

FALSTAFF

Talk of the devil!   Alla malora!

QUICKLY

She's at the door although I tried to stop E vuol passar e la trattengo a stento ...
  her ...

FALSTAFF

Where can I hide me?   Dove m'ascondo?

ALICE

Go behind the screen.   Dietro il paravento.

(Falstaff conceals himself behind the screen. When he is hidden, Quickly signals to Meg, who is outside the right-hand door, to enter. Meg enters, feigning alarm. Quickly goes out again.)

MEG

Oh Alice! What confusion!   Alice! che spavento!
And uproar! What a scandal!   Che chiasso! Che discordia!
Don't waste a single moment.   Non perdere un momento.
Hurry!   Fuggi! ...

ALICE

For heaven's sake!   Misericordia!
What's happened?   Che avvenne?

MEG

Your husband's coming,   Il tuo consorte
Shouting: "Just let me catch him!" Vien gridando "accorr'uomo!"
Swearing ...   Dice ...

ALICE
(quickly, sotto voce)

(Speak a bit louder.)	(Parla più forte.)

MEG

That he's intent on murder!	Che vuol scannare un uomo!

ALICE
(as before)

(Stop laughing.)	(Non ridere.)

MEG

Jealous rage	Ei correva
Consumes him and he swears	Invaso de tremendo
He's betrayed! And he is cursing	Furor! Maledicendo
All womankind as faithless!	Tutte le figlie d'Eva!

ALICE

Now heaven help me!	Misericordia!

MEG

He declares that you hide a lover;	Dice che un tuo ganzo hai nascosto;
He'll find the man and skin him	Lo vuole ad ogni costo
Alive ...	Scoprir ...

QUICKLY
(re-entering, very frightened, and shouting move loudly than before)

O Mistress Alice!	Signora Alice!
Here's Master Ford! Now save yourself!	Vien Mastro Ford! Salvatevi!
He's raging like a tempest!	È come una tempesta!
Thundering, roaring, bellowing;	Strepita, tuona, fulmina,
He strikes his brow in fury,	Si dà dei pugni in testa,
None can escape his fury ...	Scoppia in minaccie ed urla ...

ALICE
(approaching Quickly; in a low voice, a little frightened)

(A joke, or are you serious?)	(Dassenno oppur da burla?)

QUICKLY
(in full voice)

I'm serious. He broke the hedge down, [30]	Dassenno. Egli scavalca
He's crashing through the garden ...	Le siepi del giardino ...
With half of Windsor hard	Lo segue una gran calca
At his heels ... I hear him coming ...	De gente ... è già vicino ...
And it's too late for he is	Mentr'io vi parlo ei valca
Upon us ...	L'ingresso ...

FORD
(offstage, yelling)

Let me find him!	Malandrino!!!

FALSTAFF
(in great alarm has already taken a step to escape from the screen but on hearing Ford's voice he goes back to hide again.)

The devil comes in person	Il diavolo cavalca
To supervise my ruin!!	Sull'arco di un violino!!

(With a very quick gesture, Alice closes the screen on him so that he cannot be seen.)

Alice, Meg, Mistress Quickly, Master Ford, *then hard on his heels* **Dr Caius,** *then* **Fenton,** *then* **Bardolph** *and* **Pistol,** *then* **Nannetta. Falstaff** *invisible behind the screen.*

FORD
(shouting from the back to those who follow him)

The door must be bolted! The guard must be posted!	Chiudete le porte! Sbarrate le scale!
The boar must be hunted! The pig must be roasted!	Seguitemi a caccia! Scoviamo il cignale!

96

(Dr Caius and Fenton enter, running.)

Go look for his footprints and track him.   Correte sull'orme, sull'usta.

(to Fenton)

You look in the corridor.   Tu fruga negli anditi.

BARDOLPH and **PISTOL**
(run into the room shouting, while Fenton goes out left.)

We'll find him!   A caccia!

FORD
(to Bardolph and Pistol, pointing to the room on the right)

The beast won't escape us!   Sventate la fuga!

Go look in the bedroom!   Cercate là dentro!

(Bardolph and Pistol rush into the room with raised sticks.)

ALICE
(confronting Ford)

Are you out of your senses?   Sei tu dissennato?

What's wrong?   Che fai?

FORD
(seeing the basket)

What's there? What's in the basket?   Chi c'è dentro quel cesto?

ALICE

Dirty linen.   Il bucato.

FORD

Then wash it my lady!   Ni lavi!! rea moglie!

(giving a bunch of keys to Dr Caius, who goes out left, running)

Here, take all the keys   Tu, piglia le chiavi,

And go search in the closets!   Rovista le casse, va.

(turning back to Alice)

Wash it in public!   Ben tu mi lavi!

(He kicks the basket.)

To hell with the linen!   Al diavolo i cenci!

(shouting to the back)

Be sure that the park gate   Sprangatemi l'uscio

Is guarded!   Del parco!

(He furiously pulls out the laundry from the basket, rummaging and searching inside, and scattering all the contents on the floor.)

My collars . . . a nightdress . . . I shall Find you at last! Greasy napkins! Ugh! Ugh! Dirty stockings! I'll find you, – And dishcloths . . . and smelly old nightcaps . . . Not there! . . .

– Camicie . . . gonnelle . . .–Or ti sguscio, Briccon! – Strofinacci! Via! Via! Cuffie rotte! – Ti scugio. – Lenzuola . . . berretti da notte . . . – Non c'è . . .

(He overturns the basket.)

ALICE, MEG, QUICKLY
(looking at the scattered laundry)

What confusion!   Che uragano!!

FORD
(shouting and running, exit left)

Go search every bedroom,   Cerchiam sotto il letto,

The kitchen, the pantry, the oven, the chimney,   Nel forno, nel pozzo, nel bagno, sul tetto,

And the cellar . . .   In cantina . . .

ALICE

He's a lunatic!   È farnetico!

QUICKLY

Now's the moment.   Cogliam tempo.

ALICE

But how'll he   Troviamo

Ever make his exit?   Modo com'egli esca.

In the basket.   Nel panier.

ALICE

No, he'd never   No, là dentro
Get in it, the man's enormous.   Non c'entra, è troppo grosso.

FALSTAFF
(*Bewildered, he hears Alice's words, appears and runs to the basket.*)

Let's try. Yes, perfect, perfect.   Vediam; sì, c'entro, c'entro.

ALICE

I'll go and call the servants.   Corro a chiamare i servi.
(*Exit.*)

MEG
(*to Falstaff, pretending surprise*)

Sir John! You here? You?   Sir John! Voi qui? Voi?

FALSTAFF
(*getting into the basket*)

I love you!   T'amo!
Meg, I adore you . . . Rescue me! Rescue   Amo te sola . . . salvami! salvami!
me!

QUICKLY
(*to Falstaff, while gathering up the linen*)

Hurry!   Svelto!

MEG

Hurry!   Lesto!

MEG, QUICKLY

Push him!   Svelto!

FALSTAFF
(*cramming himself with a great effort into the basket*)

Ahi! . . . Ahi! . . . I'm in . . . Now cover   Ahi! . . . Ahi! . . . Ci sto . . . Copritemi . . .
me . . .

QUICKLY
(*to Meg*)

Hurry! We'll fill the basket.   Presto! colmiamo il cesto.
(*Between them, with great haste, they pile the laundry back into the basket.*)

While **Meg** and **Quickly** are busy hiding **Falstaff** under the laundry, **Nannetta** and
Fenton enter from the left.

NANNETTA
(*to Fenton, sotto voce and cautiously*)

Come here.   Vien qua.

FENTON

What madness!   Che chiasso!

NANNETTA
(*approaching the screen; Fenton follows*)

House filled with brawling!   Quanti schiamazzi!
Love's hand will guide us.   Segui il mio passo.

FENTON

Love's voice is calling!   Casa di pazzi!

NANNETTA

Madness all round us,   Qui ognun delira
Madness above.   Con vario error.
They're mad with fury . . .   Son pazzi d'ira . . .

FENTON

And we with love.   E noi d'amor.

NANNETTA
(*She takes him by the hand, leads him behind the screen and there they hide.*)

Follow me. But quietly.   Seguimi. Adagio.

FENTON

Now who can find us?   Nessun m'ha scorto.

NANNETTA

The screen's our shelter.   Tocchiamo il porto.

FENTON

Close it behind us.   Siamo a nostr'agio.

NANNETTA

Be quiet and careful.   Sta zitto e attento.

FENTON
(*embracing her*)

Let me caress you!   Vien sul mio petto!

NANNETTA

Screen that protects us,   Il paravento
Fondly we bless you!   Sia benedetto!

Nannetta and **Fenton** *are concealed behind the screen.* **Ford** *and* **Dr Caius** *enter from the left,* **Bardolph, Pistol** *and the townspeople from the right.* **Quickly** *and* **Meg** *are beside the basket in which* **Falstaff** *is hidden. Later,* **Alice** *returns at the back.*

DR CAIUS
(*shouting, offstage*)

The villain!   Al ladro!

FORD
(*likewise*)

Find the traitor!   Al pagliardo!

DR CAIUS
(*enters, running across the room*)

I'll slaughter him!   Squartatelo!

FORD
(*likewise*)

And kill him!   Al ladro!
(*They meet Bardolph and Pistol entering from the right.*)

There?   C'è?

PISTOL

No.   No.

FORD
(*to Bardolph*)

There?   C'è?

BARDOLPH

Not there, no.   Non c'è, no.

FORD
(*running about, searching everywhere and rummaging in the chest-seat*)

I'll tear the whole house   Vado a soqquadro
To pieces.   La casa.

(*Bardolph and Pistol exeunt left.*)

DR CAIUS
(*having looked up the chimney*)

He's not in the chimney.   Non trovo nessuno.

FORD

And yet somewhere   Eppur giuro
That villain is hiding. I know it,   Che l'uomo è qua dentro. Ne sono sicuro!
I know it! I know it!   Sicuro! Sicuro!

DR CAIUS

Sir John! I shall laugh
On the day when I see you strung high on the
    gallows!

Sir John! Sarò gaio
Quel dì ch'io ti veda dar calci a rovaio!

FORD
(hurling himself at the wardrobe and trying to wrench it open)

Come out now, you scoundrel! Or I'll break
Every panel!

Vien fuora, furfante! T'arrendi! O bombardo
Le mura!

DR CAIUS
(trying to open the wardrobe with the keys)

Surrender!

T'arrendi!

FORD

Come out now! You coward!
Old lecher!

Vien fuora! Codardo!
Sugliardo!

BARDOLPH *and* PISTOL

Can't find him!

Nessuno!

FORD
(to Bardolph and Pistol, while he and Dr Caius continue to struggle with the wardrobe)

Go on with your searching!

Cercatelo ancora!

(Bardolph and Pistol go back where they came from.)

Surrender! I've caught you!

T'arrendi! Scanfardo!

(He finally succeeds in opening the wardrobe.)

Not there!!

Non c'è!!

DR CAIUS
(opening the chest-seat)

Come out now!

Non c'è!

Vieni fuora!

(running about the room, searching at random)

Rotten medlar! Balloon! Have a care!

Pappalardo! Beòn! Bada a te!

FORD
(Like someone obsessed he even opens the drawer of the little table.)

You scoundrel! Fat villain! Beware!

Scagnardo! Falsardo! Briccon!!

(During the uproar, Nannetta and Fenton, behind the screen, have been exchanging tender endearments. Now, as it dies down for a moment, all hear the sound of a kiss from behind the screen.)

NANNETTA *and* FENTON
(They kiss.)

*(kiss)

*(bacio)

FORD
(under his breath, staring at the screen)

There!

C'è.

DR CAIUS
(likewise)

There!

C'è.

*(There follow three independent but simultaneous dialogues: **Ford** and **Dr Caius**, soon joined by **Bardolph, Pistol,** and the townspeople, gather round the screen. Behind it, **Nannetta** and **Fenton,** oblivious of all but one another, murmur tenderly. Beside the laundry basket, **Meg** and **Quickly** try to keep its occupant quiet.)*

Around the screen
FORD
(slowly and cautiously, approaching the screen)

When I catch you ...

Se t'agguanto!

DR CAIUS
(likewise)

When I seize you ...

Se ti piglio!

100

FORD

I'll despatch you!   Se t'acciuffo!

DR CAIUS

I will squeeze you!   Se t'acceffo!

FORD

I will thrash you!   Ti sconquasso!

DR CAIUS

I will beat you   T'arronciglio
Like a dog!   Come un can!

FORD

And I will smash you!   Ti rompo il ceffo!

DR CAIUS

Now beware!   Guai a te!

FORD

Nothing can save you!   Prega il tuo santo!
Now you're trapped and you will suffer!   Guai se alfin con te m'azzuffo!
When I catch you!   Se ti piglio!

DR CAIUS

When I seize you!   Se t'agguanto!

FORD

I will despatch you!   Se t'acceffo!

DR CAIUS

I will squeeze you!   Se t'acciuffo!

BARDOLPH
(*re-entering from the left*)

He has vanished.   Non si trova.

PISTOL
(*re-entering with some of the townspeople*)

He has vanished.   Non si coglie.

FORD
(*to Bardolph, Pistol and their companions*)

Psst! . . . Come closer.   Pss . . . Qua tutti.
(*whispering with delight, indicating the screen*)
I have found him.   L'ho trovato.
He's behind that screen with Alice.   Là c'è Falstaff con mia moglie.

BARDOLPH

Bloated viper! Filthy traitor!   Sozzo can vituperato!

FORD

Quiet!   Zitto!

PISTOL *and* **DR CAIUS**

Quiet!!   Zitto!!

FORD

Abuse him later.   Urlerai dopo.
For I heard the sound of kissing.   Là s'è udito il suon d'un bacio.

BARDOLPH

We must catch the rat in action   Noi dobbiam pigliare il topo
While he's nibbling at the cheese.   Mentre sta rodendo il cacio.

FORD

Let me think. Hear my intentions,   Ragioniam. Colpo non vibro
Now my plan of battle's chosen.   Senza un piano di battaglia.

THE OTHERS

Bravo!   Bravo!

DR CAIUS

A man of huge dimensions!	Un uomo di quel calibro
He could cause a great explosion!	Con un soffio ci sbaraglia.

FORD

My attack upon the bandit –	La mia tattica maestra
Let me tell you how I've planned it.	Le sue mosse pria registra.

(to Pistol and two of his companions)

Pistol, you must lead the right wing.	Voi sarete l'ala destra,

(to Bardolph and Dr Caius)

You and I will hold the centre;	Noi sarem l'ala sinistra.

(to the others)

At my signal you must enter;	E costor con pie' gagliardo
And we'll strike like triple lightning.	Sfonderanno il baluardo.

THE OTHERS

Bravo! Bravo! Fine manoeuvre!	Bravo, bravo Generale.

DR CAIUS

When you're ready, give the signal.	Aspettiamo un tuo segnale.

FORD

(to Dr Caius, putting his ear to the screen)

Put your ear a little closer!	Senti, accosta un po' l'orecchio!
What a touching lamentation!	Che patetici lamenti!!
On that nest of tender lovebirds	Su quel nido d'usignuoli
Thunderbolts will shortly fall.	Scoppierà fra poco il tuon.

BARDOLPH

(to Pistol)

Someone whispering, lovers' voices,	E la voce della donna
Voices singing songs of love.	Che risponde al cavalier.

DR CAIUS

(to Ford, putting his ear close to the screen)

Someone whispering and I see clearly	Sento, intendo e vedo chiaro
The deceitfulness of women.	Delle femmine gl'inganni.

PISTOL

(to Bardolph)

He may sing a tender love-song	Ma fra poco il lieto gioco
Soon he'll pipe another tune.	Turberà dura lezion.
We shall end that love-sick chirping,	Egli canta, ma fra poco
He'll be singing louder soon.	Muterà la sua canzon.

NEIGHBOURS

He is captured, can't escape us,	S'egli cade più non scappa,
All is well and truly planned.	Nessun più lo può salvar.
Though the devil came to help him,	Nel tuo diavolo t'incappa;
Retribution is at hand!	Che tu possa stramazzar!

FORD

(to the others)

Quiet! To me! It is the moment.	Zitto! A noi! Quest'è il momento.
Quiet! Be careful! Be on your guard.	Zitto! Attenti! Attenti a me.

DR CAIUS

Give the sign.	Dà il segnal.

FORD

One . . . Two . . . Three . . .	Uno . . . Due . . . Tre . . .

(They upset the screen.)

DR CAIUS

Isn't him!!	Non è lui!!

Behind the screen.

NANNETTA
(to Fenton)

While all those grown-ups	Mentre quei vecchi
Threaten and thunder,	Corron la giostra,
Love fills our haven	Noi di sottecchi
With peaceful wonder.	Corriam la nostra.
Love has no ear for	L'amor non ode
Bluster or blunder,	Tuon nè bufere,
Leaves them behind and flies	Vola alle sfere
Far, far above.	Beate e gode.
And fluttering wings tell of love,	Lo spiritello
All round us.	D'amor, volteggia.

FENTON
(to Nannetta)

O my Nannetta!	Bella! ridente!
Oh, how I love you,	Oh! come pieghi
I see you smiling	Verso i miei prieghi
And you accept me!	Donnescamente!
When first I saw you	Come ti vidi
I fell in love;	M'innamorai,
And saw you smiling	E tu sorridi
Because you knew.	Perché lo sai.
Now in one dream	Già un sogno bello
Of love united . . .	D'Imene albeggia.

NANNETTA

What is this madness,	Tutto delira,
Joy mixed with sadness,	Sospiro e riso.
My lips are smiling,	Sorride il viso
And yet my heart sighs.	E il cor sospira.
Tender enchantment	Dolci richiami
Of love!	D'amor.

FENTON

Ah my beloved one!	Fra quelle ciglia
Fair eyes are smiling,	Vedo due fari
My heart beguiling,	A meraviglia
And shining bright.	Sereni e chiari.
Tell me you love me.	Dimmi se m'ami!

NANNETTA

Ah, how I love you!	Si t'amo!

FENTON

I love you!	T'amo!

(The screen falls and they are discovered in confusion.)

Around the laundry basket.

QUICKLY
(to Meg)

The porpoise may rise	Facciamo le viste
To the surface for breathing;	D'attendere ai panni;
The surface is seething,	Pur che'ei non c'inganni
I hear him protesting.	Con mosse impreviste.
His jealous suspicions	Finor non s'accorse
Have led him astray,	Di nulla; egli può
The fish in our basket	Sorprenderci forse,
Will soon get away.	Confonderci no.

MEG
(to Quickly)

Then sit on the basket,	Facciamogli siepe
We must keep him under.	Fra tanto scompiglio.
Ford's lightning and thunder	Ne' giochi il periglio
Add spice to our jesting.	È un grano di pepe.

We've taken our chances And risks we have run, But danger enhances And adds to the fun.	Il rischio è un diletto Che accresce l'ardor, Che stimola in petto Gli spiriti e il cor.

FALSTAFF
(his face surfacing)

I'm stifling!	Affogo!

QUICKLY
(puhsing him down again)

Stay under!	Sta sotto!

MEG

The porpoise is rising.	Or questi s'insorge.

QUICKLY
(crouching down to talk to Falstaff in the basket)

If anyone sees you You're done for!	Se l'altro ti scorge Sei morto.

FALSTAFF
(replying from under the laundry)

I'm choking!	Son cotto!

MEG

Stay under! Stay under!	Sta sotto! Sta sotto!

FALSTAFF
(peering out)

I'm stifling!	Che caldo!

QUICKLY

Stay hidden!	Sta sotto!

FALSTAFF

I'm choking!	Mi squaglio!

QUICKLY

Stay hidden!	Sta sotto!

MEG

Now the ruffian Wants us to fan him.	Il ribaldo Vorrebbe un ventaglio.

FALSTAFF
(pleading, his nose emerging)

No, all that I need is A moment to breathe.	Un breve spiraglio Non chiedo di più.

QUICKLY

I'll gag you unless you Are silent.	Ti metto il bivaglio Sa parli.

MEG
(pushing him down under the laundry)

Down!	Giù!

QUICKLY
(likewise)

Down!	Giù!

BOTH

Down!	Giù!

MEG
(to Quickly)

Let's talk sottovoce Observing our knight, Who grunts in the basket, Lamenting his plight.	Parliam sottovoce Guardando il Messer Che brontola e cuoce Nel nostro panier.

QUICKLY
(to Meg)

So strained and bespotted	Costui s'è infardato
With damnable deeds,	Di tanta viltà,
A dip in the river	Che darlo al bucato
Is just what he needs.	È averne pietà.

FALSTAFF
(surfacing and puffing)

Ouff . . . Horrible basket!	Ouff . . . Cesto molesto!

ALICE
(who has returned and come across to the basket)

Be quiet!	Silenzio!

FALSTAFF
(getting up)

I'm choking!	Protesto!

MEG, QUICKLY

The porpoise is restless!	Che bestia restia!

FALSTAFF
(shrieking)

For God's sake release me!	Portatemi via!

MEG, QUICKLY

He's driven nearly crazy!	È matto furibondo!

FALSTAFF
(concealing himself)

I'm dying! Please help me!	Aiuto! Aiuto!

(When the screen has been thrown down, and just after Dr Caius's "Isn't him!", a three-fold exclamation closes the triple ensemble.)

FORD, BARDOLPH, PISTOL, TOWNSPEOPLE

Can I believe it!	Sbalordimento!

ALICE, MEG, QUICKLY

A happy ending!	È il finimondo!

NANNETTA, FENTON

Ah!	Ah!

FORD
(to Nannetta, furiously)

One more rebellious woman!	Ancor nuove rivolte!

(to Fenton)

And you be on your way!	Tu va pe' fatti tuoi!
A thousand times I've told you: my	L'ho detto mille volte: costei non fa
daughter's not for you.	per voi.

(Nannetta runs off in dismay, and Fenton leaves at the back.)

BARDOLPH
(running to the centre backstage)

He's there! Stop him!	È là! Ferma!

FORD

Where?	Dove?

BARDOLPH
(running)

There!	Là!

PISTOL
(running)

There on the staircase.	Là! sulle scale.

FORD

Dismember him!	Squartatelo!

We'll catch him!   A caccia!

QUICKLY

I wish you good hunting!   Che caccia infernale!

(All the men run up the staircase at the back.)

ALICE
(ringing loudly)

Ned! Will! Tom! And Jack! Here! Hurry!   Ned! Will! Tom! Isäac! Su! Presto!
Hurry!   Presto!

(Nannetta returns with four servants and a little page.)

Take the basket and tip it	Rovesciate quel cesto
Out of the window and into the river ...	Dalla finestra nell'acqua fel fosso ...
Just by that clump of reeds	Là! presso alle giuncaie
Where you see those women washing dirty linen.	Davanti al crocchio delle lavandaie.

NANNETTA, MEG, QUICKLY

Yes, yes, yes, yes!   Si, si, si, si!

NANNETTA
(to the servants, who are finding it difficult to lift the basket)

The basket's rather heavy!   C'è dentro un pezzo grosso.

ALICE
(to the page, who then goes out by the stairs)

And you, go call my husband;   Tu chiama mio marito;
(to Meg, while Nannetta and Quickly watch the servants who have succeeded in lifting the basket)

And we'll explain how merry wives are joking.	Gli narreremo il nostro caso pazzo.
So when he sees the gallant knight asoaking	Solo al vedere il Cavalier nel guazzo.
He'll find his jealous fury is cured for ever.	D'ogni gelosa ubbia sarà guarito.

QUICKLY
(to the servants)

Heavy!   Pesa!

ALICE, MEG
(to the servants, now near the window)

Heave-ho!   Coraggio!

NANNETTA

The bottom gave a crack!   Il fondo ha fatto crac!

NANNETTA, MEG, QUICKLY

Up!   Su!

ALICE
(The basket is lifted up high.)

Victorious!   Trionfo!

NANNETTA, MEG, QUICKLY

Victorious! Ha, ha!   Trionfo! Ah, ah!

ALICE

Come watch it!   Che tonfo!

NANNETTA, MEG, QUICKLY

Come watch it!   Che tonfo!

(Ford and the other men return. Alice takes her husband by the arm and leads him to the window. The basket, Falstaff, and the laundry go tumbling out of the window.)

ALL

Patatrack!   Patatrac!

(A shout and laughter from the washerwomen outside, and great merriment onstage. Then the curtain falls rapidly.)

Act Three

Part One. *A yard. On the right the outside of the Garter Inn with the inn-sign and its motto: "Honi soit qui mal y pense". A bench by the door-way. It is sunset.*
Falstaff *then the innkeeper.*

FALSTAFF
(seated on the bench, lost in thought. Then he shakes himself, bangs on the bench with his fist and, turning towards the interior of the inn, calls for the innkeeper.)

Eh! Come to serve me!

Ehi! Taverniere!

(He returns to his gloomy meditations.) [31]

Wicked world. Villainous world. Vile world!

Mondo ladro. – Mondo rubaldo. Reo mondo!

(The innkeeper comes out.)

Worthy landlord: bring me a beaker of mulled wine.

Taverniere: un bicchier di vin caldo.

(The innkeeper takes his order and goes back inside.)

For this I lived my life of adventure, a gallant knight,
A dashing courtier, to end my days being bundled in a basket,
To be flung in the Thames with a pile of dirty linen,
As if I were a cat with ten unwanted kittens.

Io, dunque, avrò vissuto tanti anni, audace e destro
Cavaliere, per essere portato in un canestro
E gittato al canale co' pannilini biechi,
Come si fa coi gatti e i catellini ciechi.

And all that kept me floating was my resplendent belly
Else I'd have drowned. Ugly ending. Water would bloat me.

Ché se non galleggiava per me quest' epa tronfia,
Certo affogavo. Brutta morte. L'acqua mi gonfia.

Sinful world. There's no virtue left. All is declining.

Mondo reo. Non c'è più virtù. Tutto declina.

Jack, go your ways, go, go, gallant old warrior. Go on
Till they come to take you. With you there'll disappear
The last perfect, manly flower of knighthood. Day that is best forgotten!
Heaven grant me grace! I grow too portly. And my hair is greying.

Va, vecchio John, va, va per la tua via; cammina
Finché tu muoia. Allor scomparirà la vera
Virilità dal mondo. Che giornataccia nera!
M'aiuti il ciel! Impinguo troppo. Ho dei peli grigi.

(The innkeeper returns with a large beaker of mulled wine on a tray. He puts the beaker on the bench and goes back into the inn.)

I'll send this friendly potion to join the Thames inside me.

Versiamo un po' di vino nell'acqua del Tamigi.

(He sips and smacks his lips; unbuttons his waistcoat, stretches out, sips again, gradually recovering his spirits.)

That's good. To drink good wine and take one's ease in the sunshine.
Sweet employment! On the instant, wine can dispel our gloomy,
Melancholy vapours; it clears the eye and the mind, from lips
It mounts to the brain, where a merry little cricket
Is trilling; a tiny cricket that chirrups to the drinker,
Filling his heart with joy. The whole universe flashes and dances,
Soon the world around him is whirling to the sound
Of the trill! That trill pervades the world!!!

Buono. Ber del vin dolce e sbottonarsi al sole,
Dolce cosa! Il buon vino sperde le tetre fole
Dello sconforto, accende l'occhio e il pensier, dal labbro
Sale al cervel e quivi risveglia il picciol fabbro
Dei trilli; un negro grillo che vibra entro l'uom brillo.
Trilla ogni fibra in cor, l'allegro etere al trillo
Guizza e il giocondo globo squilibra una demenza
Trillante! E il trillo invade il mondo!!!

Falstaff *and* **Quickly.** *The at the back,* **Alice, Nannetta, Meg, Ford, Dr Caius** *and* **Fenton.**

QUICKLY
(curtseying and interrupting Falstaff)

O Your Worship!   Reverenza.

The lovely Alice . . .   La bella Alice . . .

FALSTAFF
(rising, with an angry outburst)

To hell with you and your lovely   Al diavolo te con Alice bella!
Alice!
I've had enough of Alice! Had far too much   Ne ho piene la bisaccie! Ne ho piene le
of Alice!   budella!

QUICKLY

Oh, you're mistaken . . .   Voi siete errato . . .

FALSTAFF

A pox on her!! For my ear-drums were   Un canchero!! Sento ancor le cornate
shattered
By that mad, yelling husband. In every   Di quell'irco geloso! Ho ancor l'ossa
limb I'm battered,   arrembate
After being twisted double, and folded in D'esser rimasto curvo, come una buona
half   lama
Like a jackknife, and bundled and trundled Di Bilbào, nello spazio d'un panierin di
in a basket!   dama!
Madmen shrieking! Laundry reeking! A   Con quel tufo! E quel caldo! Un uom della
man of my rich nature,   mia tempra,
Who's very prone to melting, and delicate Che in uno stillicidio continuo si distempra!
as butter.
Then, when they'd got me stewing and   Poi, quando fui ben cotto, rovente,
steaming, and almost gleaming,   incandescente,
I was thrown in the water. Vile rabble!!!   M'han tuffato nell'acqua. Canaglie!!!

(Alice, Meg, Nannetta, Ford, Dr Caius, and Fenton appear behind a house. First one, then another, unseen by Falstaff, spies on him, hides, returns to spy.)

QUICKLY

But she is blameless, entirely blameless.   Essa è innocente. Essa è innocente.
Do not accuse her.   Prendete abbaglio.

FALSTAFF

Off with you!!   Vattene!!

QUICKLY
(fervently)

The servants were the culprits,   La colpa è di quei fanti
The shameless varlets! And she is weeping, Malaugurati! Alice piange, urla, invoca
wailing, her saint invoking.   i santi.
Unhappy lady!! She loves you. Just read   Povera donna!! V'ama. Leggete.
this.

(She draws a letter from her pocket. Falstaff takes it and begins to read it.)

ALICE
(at the back, spying, to the others, under her breath.)

(Reading.   (Legge.

FORD
(sottovoce)

Reading.   Legge.

NANNETTA

I'm sure he will believe it.   Vedrai che ci ricasca.

ALICE

Men never learn their lesson.   L'uomo non si corregge.

MEG
(to Alice, at a hidden gesture from Quickly)

Conceal yourself.   Nasconditi.

Still reading.   Rilegge.

FORD

Still reading. We have caught him.)   Rilegge. L'esca inghiotte.)

FALSTAFF
(rereading the letter aloud, with great concentration)

"I shall wait for you at midnight, in Windsor Park.   "T'aspetterò nel parco Real, a mezzanotte.

You must come disguised as Herne, the Sable Huntsman,   Tu verrai travestito da Cacciatore nero

And at Herne's Oak, there I shall meet you."   Alla quercia di Herne."

QUICKLY

Ah! Love loves a mystery.   Amor ama il mistero.

This is the plan that Alice has made, using a strange   Per rivedervi Alice, si val d'una leggenda

Old Windsor tale. All the glade around that oak is haunted.   Popolar. Quella quercia è un luogo da tregenda.

That's where they found the Huntsman, suspended from its branches.   Il Cacciatore nero d'è impeso ad un suo ramo.

All men swear that at midnight his ghost returns . . .   V'ha chi crede vederlo ricomparir . . .

FALSTAFF
(Pacified again, he takes Quickly by the arm and leads her into the tavern.)

Let's enter.   Entriamo.

There we can talk more freely. Tell me the grisly story.   Là si discorre meglio. Narrami la tua frasca.

QUICKLY
(Beginning the story of the legend, with an air of mystery, she enters the inn with Falstaff.)

There in the darkness, on the stroke of midnight . . .   Quando il rintocco della mezzanotte . . .

Demons assemble, rising from the tomb,   Cupo si sparge nel silente orror,

Throng there to celebrate unholy mysteries . . .   Sorgon gli spirti vagabondi a frotte . . .

Alice, Meg, Nannetta, Ford, Dr Caius and **Fenton.** *Later* **Quickly.**

FORD
(from the back, during Quickly's narration)

We've caught him . . .   Ci casca . . .

ALICE
(advancing with the group, comically imitating Quickly's mysterious tone and continuing her story)

There in the darkness on the stroke of midnight,   Quando il rintocco della mezzanotte

Demons assemble, rising from the tomb;   Cupo si sparge nel silente orror,

Throng there to celebrate unholy mysteries;   Sorgon gli spirti vagabondi a frotte

Herne, the Sable Huntsman, comes stalking through the gloom.   E vien nel parco il nero Cacciator.

And he advances slowly, slowly, slowly,   Egli cammina lento, lento, lento,

A grisly spectre gliding through the darkness,   Nel gran letargo della sepoltura.

With death-white countenance . . .   S'avanza livido . . .

NANNETTA

Oh, how alarming!   Oh! che spavento!

MEG

I feel delicious shivers down my spine!   Già sento il brivido della paura!

(in her natural voice)

A fairytale that nurserymaids [32]	Fandonie che ai bamboli
Recount to their charges	Raccontan le nonne
With various embellishments	Con lunghi preamboli,
To make them sleep well!	Per farli dormir.

ALICE, NANNETTA, MEG

But after our jesting	Vendetta di donne
A new tale they'll tell.	None deve fallir.

ALICE
(resuming her narration)

With death-white countenance he stalks towards that oak-tree	S'avanaza livido e il passo converge
To stand beneath that bough where he once took his life.	Al tronco ove esalò l'anima prava.
Goblins surround him. Growing from his forehead,	Sbucan le Fate. Sulla fronte egli erge
He feels huge antlers branching, branching . . .	Due corna lunghe, lunghe, lunghe . . .

FORD

Bravo!	Brava!
When I see those huge antlers, I'll enjoy them!	Quelle corna saranno la mia gioia!

ALICE
(to Ford)

Careful! You should be punished too!	Bada! tu pur ti meriti
Daring to doubt your wife!	Qualche castigatoia!

FORD

Forgive me. Now I know I should have trusted you.	Perdona. Riconsco i miei demeriti.

ALICE

Beware if in the future	Me guai se ancor ti coglie
I once again discover	Quella mania deroce
That my husband could ever dare suspect me	Di cercar dentro il guscio d'una noce
Or dream I have a lover.	L'amante di tua moglie.
But time is pressing. Let's plan our midnight meeting.	Ma il tempo stringe e vuol fantasia lesta.

MEG

Yes indeed.	Affrettiam.

FENTON

And agree on our disguises.	Concertiam la mascherata.

ALICE

Nannetta!	Nannetta!

NANNETTA

What shall I be?	Eccola qua!

ALICE
(to Nannetta)

You'll play Titania,	Sarai la Fata
The Queen of all the Fairies. You'll wear a white veil,	Regina delle Fate, in bianca vesta
And be dressed all in white, girded with rosebuds;	Chiusa in candido vel, cinta di rose.

NANNETTA

And I can sing my song telling of fairy charms.	E canterò parole armonïose.

You must come dressed in green; nymph of the woodland.	Tu la verde sarai Ninfa silvanna,
And what disguise for Quickly? She'll make a fine witch.	E la comare Quickly una befana.

(*The stage darkens as night falls.*)

NANNETTA

Riding a broomstick!	A meraviglia!

ALICE

And Windsor lads and lasses [33]	Avrò con me dei putti
I'll bring along with me	Che fingeran folletti,
To be hobgoblins,	E spiritelli,
Tiny elves,	E diavoletti,
And impish brats	E pipistrelli,
And Boston devils.	E farfarelli.
When Falstaff arrives in cloak and antlers,	Su Falstaff camufato in manto e corni
We'll set upon him roundly ...	Ci scaglieremo tutti ...

NANETTA, MEG, FENTON

Roundly, soundly!	Tutti! Tutti!

ALICE

And teaching him a lesson	E lo tempesteremo
We'll force him to confession	Finch'abbia confessata
Of all his wicked ways.	La sua perversita.
Then we shall take our masks off	Poi ci smaschereremo
And long before it's morning	E, pria che il ciel raggiorni,
We can lead him back to Windsor,	La giuliva brigata
Gaily returning home.	Se ne ritornerà.

MEG

It's sunset. Let's go in.	Vien sera. Rincasiam.

ALICE

And meet again	L'appuntamento
By the oaktree at midnight.	È alla quercia di Herne.

FENTON

We'll do so.	È inteso.

NANNETTA

Oh, how delightful!	A meraviglia!
What a marvellous adventure!	Oh! che allegro spavento!

ALICE, NANNETTA, FENTON
(*taking their leave*)

Till midnight.	Addio.

MEG
(*to Nannetta and Alice*)

Till midnight.	Addio.

(*Alice, Nannetta and Fenton go off to the left, Meg to the right.*)

ALICE
(*far left, calling to Meg, who is already offstage right*)

Will you provide the lanterns?	Provvedi le lanterne.

MEG

Yes.	Si.

(*As they go out, Quickly comes out of the inn and, seeing Ford and Dr Caius in conversation, remains in the doorway to eavesdrop.*) [34]

FORD
(to Dr Caius, speaking in a low voice, close to the inn)

Now there's no doubt, soon you shall wed my daughter.

Non dubitar, tu sposerai mia figlia.

Can you remember the dress that she'll be wearing?

Rammenti bene il suo travestimento?

DR CAIUS

Girded with rosebuds, white her veil and her garments.

Cinta di rose, il vel bianco e la vesta.

ALICE
(calling from offstage left)

Do not forget the masks we need.

Non ti scordar le maschere.

MEG
(calling from offstage right)

I'll bring them.
And you rehearse the children.

No, certo.
Né tu le raganelle!

FORD
(continuing his conversation with Dr Caius)

Now let me tell you
My plan of action. When the masquerade is ended,

Io già disposi
Le rete mia. Sul finir della festa

You'll lead her to me, with both your faces hidden,

Verrete a me col volto ricoperto

Hers by the veil, yours in the hood you're wearing.

Essa dal vel, tu da un mantel fratesco

And I shall bless you both, bride and bridegroom.

E vi benedirò come due sposi.

DR CAIUS
(taking Ford's arm and starting to leave on the left)

She'll be mine then!

Siam d'accordo.

QUICKLY
(in the doorway, making a sly gesture at the pair as they leave)

(Don't be certain!)
(She leaves right, rapidly, and then calls from offstage, moving ever further away.)

(Stai fresco!)

Nannetta! Eh! Nannetta!
Nannetta! Eh!

Nannetta! Ohé! Nannetta!
Nannetta! Ohé!

NANNETTA
(offstage left, her voice receding in the distance)

What now? What now?

Che c'è? Che c'è?

QUICKLY
(as before)

Be ready with that fairy song I taught you.

Prepara la canzone della Fata.

NANNETTA
(as before)

I know it well.

È preparata.

ALICE
(offstage left)

And don't be late.

Tu, non tardar.

QUICKLY
(offstage right, still farther away)

The first to arrive will wait there.

Chi prima arriva, aspetta.

Part Two. *Windsor Park. In the middle the mighty oaktree of Herne the Hunter. At the back, the bank of a ditch. Dense foliage. Flowering shrubs. Night.*

The park rangers' horns are heard in the distance. Gradually, the park is lit by the rays of the moon.

Fenton, *then* **Nannetta** *disguised as the Fairy Queen,* **Alice,** *undisguised, with a monk's hood over her arm and holding a mask.* **Mistress Quickly,** *with a witch's cap and great cloak, a broomstick, and a snout mask in her hand. Then* **Meg,** *disguised in green veils.*

FENTON

From lover's lips a tender song is stealing, [35]	Dal labbro il canto estasîato vola
Through the shadows how ardently it flies on;	Pe' silenzi notturni e va lontano
He sets it winging through the silent darkness,	E alfin ritrova un altro labbro umano
Until a second voice returns the love-song.	Che gli risponde colla sua parola.
And when the lover hears that voice replying,	Allor la nota che non è più sola
His heart is filled with sudden joy and yearning,	Vibra di gioia in un accordo arcano
And all the moonlight seems to be trembling	E innamorando l'aer antelucano
To hear that new voice as it softly enchants all.	Come altra voce al suo fonte rivola.
Echo makes sweet reply, but then the lover	Quivi ripiglia suon, ma la sua cura
Grows impatient once more; still he's divided.	Tende sempre ad unir chi lo disuna.
He would unite his lips to those that answer.	Così baciai la disîata bocca!
"Bocca baciata non perde ventura."	"Bocca baciata non perde ventura."

NANNETTA
(offstage, distant, drawing nearer)

"Anzi rinnova come fa la luna."   "Anzi rinnova come fa la luna."

FENTON
(turning impetuously in the direction the voice came from)

The singing dies when lips can be united.   Ma il canto muor nel bacio che lo tocca.

(Nannetta enters; they embrace.)

ALICE
(coming between Fenton and Nannetta, and making him put on the black habit)

None of that sir! Put on this monkish habit.   Nossignore! Tu indossa questa cappa.

FENTON
(as Alice and Nannetta help him to don the robe)

But why a monk?   Che vuol dir ciò?

NANNETTA
(adjusting the hood)

Do as you're told, sir!   Lasciati fare.

ALICE
(handing Fenton a mask)

This mask too.   Allaccia.

NANNETTA
(looking him over)

A little Trappist monk who means to trap me!   È un fraticel sgusciato dalla Trappa.

ALICE
(hurriedly helping Fenton to don his mask)

That clever trick Master Ford is preparing	Il tradimento che Ford ne minaccia
Will be turned inside out to your advantage.	Tornar deve in suo scorno e in nosto aiuto.

FENTON

Explain to me.   Spiegatevi.

ALICE

Just obey my orders and trust me.   Ubbidisci presto e muto.

113

A chance like this won't come again, so take it.	L'occasîone come viene scappa.

(to Quickly)

Whom did you choose to play the bride?	Chi vestirai da finta sposa?

QUICKLY

A rascally,	Un gaio
Red-nosed knave who detests our Doctor Caius.	Ladron nasuto che aborre il Dottor Cajo.

MEG
(running on from the back, to Alice)

I've concealed all the children in the forest. We're ready.	Ho nascosto i folletti lungo il fosso. Siam pronte.

ALICE
(listening closely)

Quiet. Sound of heavy footsteps!	Zitto. Viene il pezzo grosso.
Vanish!	Via! . . .

(The women and Fenton go off to the left.)

Falstaff with a pair of antlers on his head, wrapped in an ample cloak. Then **Alice.** Then **Meg.** Midnight is striking as Falstaff comes onstage. [36]

FALSTAFF

One, two, three, four, five, six, seven striking,	Una, due, tre, quattro, cinque, sei, sette botte,
Eight, nine, ten, eleven, twelve o'clock. It is midnight.	Otto, nove, dieci, undici, dodici. Mezzanotte.
Here is the oak-tree. Gods on high protect me now! Hear me,	Quest'è la quercia. Numi, proteggetemi! Giove!
Jove, who became a bull out of love for fair Europa!	Tu per amor d'Europa ti trasformasti in bove;
You bore the horns too. And proudly I follow your example.	Portasti corna. I numi c'insegnan la modestia.
By love's own metamorphosis a man is soon made beastly.	L'amore metamorfosa un uom in una bestia.

(listening)

There is her gentle footstep!	Odo un soave passo!

(Alice appears at the back.)

My Alice! Your lover calls you!	Alice! Amor ti chiama!

(approaching her)

Join me! With love I'm burning!	Vieni! l'amor m'infiamma!

ALICE
(approaching Falstaff)

Sir John!	Sir John!

FALSTAFF

You are my dear one!	Sei la mia dama!

ALICE

Sir John!	Sir John!

FALSTAFF
(seizing her)

Behold your deer!	Se le mia damma!

ALICE

A witty deer, forsooth!	A sfavillante amor!

FALSTAFF
(ardently clasping her)

Join me! Love is in season!	Vieni! Già fremo e fervo!

ALICE
(trying to avoid his embrace)

Sir John!	Sir John!

You are my roe!
I am your stag waiting to gore you.
Let the sky rain potatoes, cabbages, and
turnips!
    Together we'll devour them!
    And love will triumph!
    Alone here . . .

Sono il tuo servo!
Sono il tuo cervo imbizzarrito. Ed or
Piovan tartufi, rafani e finocchi!!!

E sien la mia pastura!
E amor trabocchi!
Siam soli . . .

ALICE

No. There in the dark behind me
Is Mistress Meg.

No. Qua nella selva densa
Mi segue Meg.

FALSTAFF

    She doubles my adventure!
She may come too. Divide me then!
Carve up my joints between you!!
Dismember me! The God of Love
At last rewards me!
I love you! I love you!

È doppia l'avventura!
Venga anche lei! Squartatemi
Come un camoscio a mensa!!
Sbranatemi!!! Cupido.
Alfin mu ricompensa.
Io t'amo! t'amo!

MEG
(offstage)

Oh help me!!!

Aiuto!!!

ALICE
(feigning alarm)

    Who's screaming?
Alas!

Un grido!
    Ahimè!

MEG
(at the back, not coming forward, and not masked)

The wicked goblins!

Vien la tregenda!

(She runs off.)

ALICE
(again feigning alarm)

    Alas! Escape them!

Ahimè. Fuggiamo!

FALSTAFF
(alarmed)

Save me!

Dove?

ALICE
(rushing off to the right)

For all my sins may heaven forgive me!

Il cielo perdoni al mio peccato!

FALSTAFF
(flattening himself against the trunk of the oak)

The devil cannot wish for my damnation.

Il diavolo non vuol ch'io sia dannato.

NANNETTA
(offstage)

Fairies! Goblins! Sylphides! Water-
nymphs! And wood-nymphs!
Hear me! Our magic star has risen, your
Queen commands you.

Ninfe! Elfi! Silfi! Doridi! Sirene!

L'astro degli incantesmi in cielo è sorto.

(She appears at the back amid the foliage)

Arise now! Sprites of the woodland!

Sorgete! Ombre serene!

WOMEN'S VOICES

Wood nymphs, sylphides, give answer.

Ninfe! Silfe! Sirene!

FALSTAFF
(throwing himself full-length on the ground face downwards)

Those are the fairies. He must die who sees
them.

Sono le Fate. Chi le guarda è morto.

Enter **Nannetta** as the Fairy Queen, **Alice**, *and some girls dressed as white fairies and blue fairies.* **Falstaff** *still lying on the ground, face down, motionless.*

ALICE
(coming forward cautiously from the left with some fairies)

Follow me.   Inoltriam.

NANNETTA
(advancing from the left with other fairies and noticing Falstaff)

He is there.   Egli è là.

ALICE
(She sees Falstaff and points him out to the others.)

Lying low.   Steso al suol.

NANNETTA

He is frozen   Lo confonde

With fear.   Il terror.

(They all advance cautiously.)

FAIRIES

He is hiding.   Si nasconde.

ALICE

Do not laugh!   Non ridiam!

FAIRY CHORUS

We'll not laugh!   Non ridiam!

NANNETTA
(indicating their places to the fairies, while Alice goes off quickly to the left)

Gather round in a ring,   Tutte qui, dietro a me.

And begin.   Cominciam.

FAIRY CHORUS

You begin.   Tocca a te.

(The little fairies gather in a ring around their Queen. The bigger fairies form a group on the left.)

THE FAIRY QUEEN

On breath of zephyrs softly borne,	Sil fil d'un soffio etesio
A gentle song is calling,	Scorrete, agili larve;
Under the boughs, on silent lawn,	Fra i rami un baglior cesio
Silvery rays are falling.	D'alba lunare apparve.

We'll dance now! At my command you	Danzate! e il passo blando
Must quietly dance and sing,	Mizuri un blando suon,
Marking the beat with gentle feet,	Le magiche accoppiando
To form our magic ring.	Carole alla canzon.

FAIRY CHORUS

The forest slumbers, the leafy grove	La selva dorme e sperde
Is silent, and seems	Incenso ed ombra; e par
A magic grotto, a cavern	Nell'aer denso un verde
Lost in watery dreams.	Asilo in fondo al mar.

THE FAIRY QUEEN

We wander through the moonlight,	Erriam sotto la luna
Enchanted flowers we gather,	Scegliendo fior da fiore,
Reading the secret writing	Ogni corolla in core
Hidden in every blossom.	Porta la sua fortuna.
With woodbine, violets, and lilies	Coi gigli e le vïole
We weave our soft enchantment,	Scriviam de' nomi arcani,
Spelling our words with sweet blooms,	Dalle fatate mani
And telling our secret story.	
Purple and blue and emerald,	Germoglino parole,
Lilies of white and gold,	Parole alluminate
Gently we twine them. With flowers	Di puro argento e d'ôr,
Our fairy secrets are told.	Carmi e malie. Le Fate
	Hanno per cifre i fior.

116

THE FAIRY CHORUS
(while the little fairies go gathering flowers)

We move from flower to flower,	Moviam ad una ad una
Pass over frond and fern;	Sotto il lunare albor,
Let us approach that oak-tree	Verso la quercia bruna
Sacred to hunter Herne.	Del nero Cacciator.

(As they sing, all the fairies and their Queen advance slowly towards the oak.)

───────────────

From the back, at the left, there emerge: **Alice** *in disguise;* **Meg** *as a green nymph, masked;* **Mistress Quickly** *as a witch, masked. They are preceded by* **Bardolph** *wearing a red habit, not masked but with the hood pulled down over his face, and* **Pistol** *as a satyr. There follow:* **Dr Caius** *in a grey habit, not masked;* **Fenton** *in a black habit, masked; and* **Ford** *neither in a habit nor masked. Various townspeople in fantastic costumes bring up the procession and go to form a group on the right. At the back, other masqueraders carry lanterns of various forms.*

BARDOLPH
(stumbling over Falstaff's body and stopping the procession with an emphatic gesture)

What is this? Alto là!

PISTOL
(running up)

Who is there? Chi va là?

FALSTAFF

Alas? Pietà!

QUICKLY
(prodding Falstaff with her broomstick)

A mortal! C'è un uomo!

ALICE, NANNETTA, MEG

A man! C'è un uomo!

FAIRY CHORUS

A man! Un uom!

FORD
(who has come up close to Falstaff)

He's horned with branching antlers! Cornuto come un bue!

PISTOL

He's fat and round as a pumpkin! Rotondo come un pomo!

BARDOLPH

Broad and wide as a galleon! Grosso come una nave!

BARDOLPH, PISTOL
(prodding Falstaff with their feet)

Mortal man, arise! Alzati, olà!

FALSTAFF
(lifting his head)

I fear a crane is needed! Portatemi una grue!
I cannot. Non posso.

FORD

He's far too heavy. È troppo grave.

QUICKLY

And corrupted! È corrotto!

FAIRY CHORUS

He's corrupted! È corrotto!

ALICE, NANNETTA, MEG

He's unwholesome! È impuro!

FAIRY CHORUS

He's unwholesome! È impuro!

117

BARDOLPH
(gesticulating like a wizard)

A magic spell is called for!	Si faccia lo scongiuro!

ALICE
(aside, to Nannetta, while Dr Caius is evidently trying to find someone. Fenton and Quickly hide Nannetta behind them.)

(Time that you went into hiding.   (Evita il tuo periglio,
You must escape Doctor Caius.   Già il Dottor Cajo ti cerca.

NANNETTA

We'll slip behind that thicket.   Troviamo un nascondiglio.

(Shielded by Alice and Mistress Quickly, she and Fenton slip off at the back.)

QUICKLY

But hurry back to join us when I call you.)   Poi tornerete lesti al mio richiamo.)

BARDOLPH
(continuing his exorcism around Falstaff's body)

Little demons! Hobgoblins!   Spiritelli! Folletti!
Jack o' Lanterns! And vampires! Gnats Farfarelli! Vampiri! Agili insetti
  and mosquitoes
From the marshy inferno! Sting and stickle   Del palude infernale! Punzecchiatelo!
  him!
Tweak him and tickle him!   Orticheggiatelo!
Pinch him and prickle him!   Martirizzatelo
Bite him to pieces!   Coi grifi aguzzi!

(Some children dressed as imps run forward quickly, and fling themselves at Falstaff. From various sides, more imps, sprites, devils emerge. Some shake rattles; some have osier branches in their hands; many are carrying little red lanterns.)

FALSTAFF
(to Bardolph)

Alas! that sorcerer   Ahimè! tu puzzi
Stinks like a polecat.   Come una puzzola.

SPRITES AND DEVILS
(rolling Falstaff over to the front of the stage)

Rumble him, tumble him, rumble   Ruzzola, ruzzola, ruzzola, ruzzola!
  him, tumble him!

ALICE, MEG, QUICKLY

Prickety, prickety,   [37]   Pizzica, pizzica,
Prickety, prockety,   Pizzica, stuzzica,
Stickety, stickety,   Spizzica, spizzica,
Stickety, stockety,   Pungi, spilluzzica,
Making him cry!   Finch'egli abbài!

FALSTAFF

Ahi! Ahi! Ahi! Ahi!   Ahi! Ahi! Ahi! Ahi!

SPRITES AND DEVILS

We'll beat him and batter him,   Scrolliam crepitacoli,
And tear him and tatter him!   Scarandole e nacchere!
We'll clout him and clatter him   Di schizzi e di zacchere
And strike him and shatter him.   Quell'otre si macoli.
We'll trample and tread on him,   Maniam scorribandole,
And jump on his belly;   Danziamo la tresca,
We'll pour boiling lead on him   Treschiam le faràndole
And pound him to jelly!   Sull'ampia ventresca.
Mosquitoes and midges   Zanzare ed assilli,
Come add to his trouble,   Volate alla lizza
And sting him and prick him   Coi dardi e gli spilli!
Until he sees double!   Ch'ei crepi di stizza,
He'll burst like a bubble –   Ch'ei crepi di stizza,
A bubble that goes: Pop!   Ch'ei crepi, ch'ei crepi!

ALICE, MEG, QUICKLY

ALICE, MEG, QUICKLY

We'll grab at him, goad him,
Until we explode him.

Ch'ei crepi di stizza,
Ch'ei crepi di pizzica!

FAIRY CHORUS

Prickety, prickety,
Prickety, prockety,
Stickety, stickety,
Stickety, stockety,
Making him cry!

Pizzica, pizzica,
Pizzica, stuzzica,
Spizzica, spizzica,
Pungi, spilluzzica,
Finch'egli abbài!

FALSTAFF

Ahi! Ahi! Ahi! Ahi!

Ahi! Ahi! Ahi! Ahi!

ALICE, MEG, QUICKLY, IMPS, FAIRY CHORUS

Tickle him, tackle him,
Bump him and thump on him!
Mingle him, mangle him,
Jab him and jump on him!
Bash him and thrash him and fasten your jaws in him!
Prickle him, tickle him, sharpen your claws in him!

Cozzalo, aizzalo,
Dai pie' al cocuzzolo!
Strozzalo, strizzalo!
Gli svampi l'uzzolo!
Pizzica, pizzica, l'unghia rintuzzola!

Ruzzola, ruzzola, ruzzola, ruzzola!

DR CAIUS, FORD

Buffoon!

Cialtron!

BARDOLPH, PISTOL

Buffoon!

Poltron!

DR CAIUS, FORD

Baboon!

Ghiotton!

BARDOLPH, PISTOL

Baboon!

Pancion!

DR CAIUS, FORD

Balloon!

Bèon!

BARDOLPH, PISTOL

Balloon!

Briccon!

DR CAIUS, FORD, BARDOLPH, PISTOL

We'll make you burst!

In ginocchion!

(*The four of them together force Falstaff to rise to his knees.*)

FORD

Paunch like a pumpkin!

Pancia ritronfia!

ALICE

Brain of a bumpkin!

Guancia rigonfia!

BARDOLPH

Greatest of gluttons!

Sconquassa-letti!

QUICKLY

Burster of buttons!

Spacca-farsetti!

PISTOL

Breaker of benches!

Vuota-barilli!

MEG

Chaser of wenches!

Sfonda-sedili!

DR CAIUS

Infamous brawler!

Sfianca-giumenti!

FORD

Triple-chinned sprawler!

Triplice mento!

Say you repent it!   Di' che ti penti!
(Bardolph, who has taken Quickly's broomstick, whacks Falstaff.)

FALSTAFF

I do repent it!   Ahi! Ahi! mi pento!

ALL THE MEN

We're unrelenting!   Uom frodolento!
(Pistol, who has taken the stick from Bardolph, whacks Falstaff.)

FALSTAFF

I do repent it!   Ahi! Ahi! mi pento!

ALL THE MEN

Are you repenting?   Uom turbolento!
(Bardolph takes the stick back and whacks Falstaff once more.)

FALSTAFF

I do repent it!   Ahi! Ahi! mi pento!

ALL THE MEN

Buffoon!   Capron!
Baboon!   Scroccan!
Balloon!   Spaccon!

FALSTAFF

I swoon!   Perdon!

BARDOLPH
(his face very close to Falstaff's)

Your load of sins is mighty!   Riforma la tua vita!

FALSTAFF

You stink of acqua-vitae!   Tu puti d'acquavita.

ALL THE WOMEN

Chasten his spirit, Lord, we pray!   Domine fallo casto!

FALSTAFF

But do not let me waste away!   Ma salvagli l'addomine.

ALL THE WOMEN

Purge him of evil, Lord, we pray!   Domine fallo guasto!

FALSTAFF

But do not let me waste away!   Ma salvagli l'addomine.

ALL THE WOMEN

Cleanse his offences, Domine!   Fallo punito Domine!

FALSTAFF

But do not let me waste away!   Ma salvagli l'addomine.

ALL THE WOMEN

Make him repentant, Domine!   Fallo pentito Domine!

FALSTAFF

But do not let me waste away!   Ma salvagli l'addomine.

THE FOUR MEN

Huge globe of sinful grease,   Globo d'impurità!
Give answer.   Rispondi.

FALSTAFF

I agree.   Ben mi sta.

THE FOUR MEN

Lustful as you're obese!   Monte d'obesità!
Give answer.   Rispondi.

FALSTAFF

I agree.   Ben mi sta.

Huge human cask of sherry,
Give answer.

Otre di malvasia!
Rispondi.

FALSTAFF

I confess it.

Cosi sia.

BARDOLPH

Man who's all belly!

Re dei panciuti!

FALSTAFF

Get back, you're smelly.

Va via, tu puti.

BARDOLPH

Horned lump of jelly!

Re dei cornuti!

FALSTAFF

Get back, you're smelly.

Va via, tu puti.

THE FOUR MEN

We mean to beat you!

Furfanteria!

FALSTAFF

No! I entreat you.

Ahi! Cosi sia.

THE FOUR MEN

We mean to beat you!

Gagliofferia!

FALSTAFF

No! I entreat you.

Ahi! Cosi sia.

BARDOLPH

Satan will roast you for dinner and
eat you!!

Ed or che il diavolo ti porti via!!!

(*In the vehemence of his utterance his hood falls back.*)

FALSTAFF
(*getting up*)

Thunder and lightning!! Brimstone!!!
By my beard, this is Bardolph!

Nitro! Catrame! Solfo!!
Riconosco Bardolfo!

(*whirling on him violently*)

Nose of carnation!
Nose of damnation!
Lantern of lechery!
Beacon of treachery!
Salamander! Ignis fatuus! Dirty and dusty!
Redolent
And rusty! A stinking herring! A son of
Satan!
A vampire! Hot from Hades!
Glowing cinder! You scoundrel!
Dixisti! Truth I have spoken;
If what I've said's untrue, my belt be broken!

Naso vermiglio!
Naso bargiglio!
Puntùta lesina!
Vampa di resina!
Salamandra! Ignis fatuus! Vecchia alabarda!
Stecca
Di sartore! Schildion d'inferno! Aringa
secca!
Vampiro! Basilisco!
Manigoldo! Ladrone!
Ho detto. E se mentisco
Voglio che me si spacchi il cinturone!!!

ALL

Well spoken!

Bravo!

FALSTAFF

I'll rest for a moment. I am weary.

Un poco di pausa. Sono stanco.

QUICKLY
(*sotto voce to Bardolph, with whom she then disappears behind the trees*)

(Come now. It's time to don your bridal
garments.)

(Vieni. Ti coprirò con velo bianco.)

FORD
(*with an ironic bow to Falstaff, approaching him*)

And now, while you recover your
composure,
Sir John, tell me: tell me who wears
The horns?

Ed or, mentre vi passa la scalmana,

Sir John, dite: Il cornuto
Chi è?

ALICE *and* MEG
(approaching Falstaff)

Come tell: say who?   Chi è? Chi è?

ALICE
(unmasking)

Are you ashamed to answer?   Vi siete fatto muto?

FALSTAFF
(after a moment of bewilderment, advancing to shake Ford's hand)

Ah Master Brook, I greet you!   Caro signor Fontana!

ALICE
(coming between them)

I fear you are mistaken.   Sbagliate nel saluto.
This is Ford, he's my husband.   Questo è Ford, mio marito.

QUICKLY
(returning)

O Your Worship! . . .   Cavaliero! . . .

FALSTAFF

O Your Worship!!   Cavaliero!!

QUICKLY

Did you think these two ladies quite so   Voi credeste due donne cosi grulle,
    stupid,
And so deluded,   Così citrulle,
To risk body and soul for your attractions;   Da darsi anima e corpo all'Avversiero,
Sigh for an old man, such a greasy, gross   Per un uom vecchio, sùdicio ed obeso . . .
    man . . .

MEG, QUICKLY

A bleary-eyed old bald man . . .   Con quella testa calva . . .

ALICE, MEG, QUICKLY

And such a fat man!   E con quel peso!!

FORD

Plainly spoken.   Parlano chiaro.

FALSTAFF

It's beginning to dawn on me,   Incomincio ad accorgermi
I've been rather an ass.   D'esser stato un somaro.

ALICE

A jackass . . . with antlers.   Un cervo . . . Un bue.

FORD

Yes, truly.   Un bue.

FORD *then* ALL

A rare old monster!   E un mostro raro!

ALL TOGETHER
(laughing)

Ha! Ha!   Ah! Ah!

FALSTAFF
(who has regained his composure)

I observe that a certain kind of person   Ogni sorta di gente dozzinale
Makes merry at my misfortune.   Mi beffa e se ne gloria;
Yet, but for me, your joke would have no   Pur, senza me, costor con tanta boria
    savour,
I'm the pinch of salt that gives the jest its   Non avrebbero un briciolo di sale.
    flavour
For I, yes I, alone cause your enjoyment.   Son'io che vi fa scaltri.
And thanks to my wit, your wits can find [38] L'arguzia mia crea l'arguzia degli altri.
    some employment.

ALL

Well spoken!   Ma bravo!

By the Gods!	Per gli Dei!
If I weren't laughing, I'd have struck you down!	Se non ridessi ti sconquasserei!
Enough now. Listen to my next proposal.	Ma basta. Ed ora vo' che m'ascoltiate.
Our masquerade deserves a royal ending,	Coronerem la mascherata bella
And I have planned one. Witness now	Cogli sponsali della
The Fairy Queen's betrothal.	Regina delle Fate.

(*Dr Caius, masked, and Bardolph, dressed as the Fairy Queen, wearing a veil, advance hand-in-hand.*) [39]

Now the Queen and her bridegroom are advancing.	Già s'avanza la coppia degli sposi.
Behold them.	Attenti!

ALL

Entrancing!	Attenti!

FORD

See her there, in white she dresses,	Eccola in bianca vesta
A virgin wreath hides her tresses,	Col velo e il serto delle rose in testa,
Standing beside her bridegroom, whom I have chosen.	E il fidanzato suo ch'io le disposi.
Make a circle round them!	Circondatela, o Ninfe.

(*Dr Caius and Bardolph stand in the centre; fairies large and small surround them.*)

ALICE
(*presenting Nannetta and Fenton who have just entered; Nannetta is entirely concealed by a large, dense blue veil. Fenton wears his mask and habit.*)

Another couple	Un'altra coppia
Of faithful tender lovers	D'amanti desiosi
Join them, standing before you	Chiede d'essere ammessa agli augurosi
Hoping that you'll also bless them!	Connubi!

FORD

So be it. We'll have a double wedding!	E sia. Farem la festa doppia.
Now bring the lanterns closer.	Avvicinate i lumi.

(*The imps, directed by Alice, bring their lanterns closer.*)

May heaven unite you!	Il ciel v'accoppia.

(*Alice takes the hand of the smallest child, who is dressed as an imp, and guides it in such a way that his lantern will light up Bardolph's face when the latter's veil is removed. Another imp, guided by Meg, lights up Nannetta and Fenton.*)

Now remove the disguises. Apotheosis!	Giù le maschere e i veli. Apoteòsi!

(*At Ford's command, Fenton and Dr Caius swiftly remove their masks. Nannetta removes her veil, and Quickly whisks Bardolph's off. All four can be seen plainly.*)

ALL
(*laughing, except for Ford and Dr Caius*)

Ha! Ha! Ha! Ha!	Ah! Ah! Ah! Ah!

DR CAIUS
(*recognising Bardolph, is rooted to the spot with surprise*)

Disaster!	Spavento!

FORD
(*astonished*)

Who betrayed me?	Tradimento!

FALSTAFF, PISTOL, CHORUS
(*laughing*)

Apotheosis!	Apoteòsi!

FORD
(*catching sight of the other couple*)

Fenton with my daughter!!!	Fenton con mia figlia!!!

DR CAIUS
(*in alarm*)

I am married to Bardolph!	Ho sposato Bardolfo!

ALL

Ha! Ha!   Ah! Ah!

DR CAIUS

Disaster!   Spavento!

ALICE, MEG, QUICKLY

We triumph!   Vittoria!

FALSTAFF, PISTOL, CHORUS

They triumph! They triumph!   Evviva! Evviva!

FORD
(reeling with surprise)

I am bewildered!   Oh! meraviglia!

ALICE
(coming up to Ford)

A man is sometimes caught in a trap   L'uom cade spesso nelle reti ordite
That he himself has prepared for others.   Dalle malizie sue.

FALSTAFF
(approaching Ford with an ironic bow)

Now, dearest Master Ford, I pray you, tell   Caro buon Messer Ford, ed ora, dite:
me:
Which of us wears the horns?   Lo scornato chi è?

FORD
(pointing to Dr Caius)

He.   Lui.

DR CAIUS
(pointing to Ford)

You.   Tu.

FORD

No.   No.

DR CAIUS

Yes.   Si.

BARDOLPH
(pointing to Ford and Dr Caius)

You.   Voi.

FENTON
(also pointing to Ford and Dr Caius)

They.   Lor.

DR CAIUS
(joining Ford)

Us.   Noi.

FALSTAFF

Both together.   Tutti e due.

ALICE
(setting Falstaff with Ford and Dr Caius)

No. All you three!   No. Tutti e tre.
(to Ford, indicating Nannetta and Fenton)
Turn to these children; such anxious   Volgiti e mira quelle ansie leggiadre.
tender pleading . . .

NANNETTA
(to Ford, clasping her hands)

Please forgive us, O father.   Perdonateci, padre.

FORD

Since it cannot be cured, I must endure it,   Chi schivare no può la propria noia
And I surrender gladly.   L'accetti di buon grado.

124

Your father gives his blessing,
And may heaven make you joyful.

Facciamo il parentado.
E che il ciel vi dia gioia.

ALL

Hurray, then!

Evviva!

FALSTAFF

A chorus now, with all united.

Un coro a terminiam la scena.

FORD

Then, with Sir John, to dine you're all
   invited.

Poi con Sir Falstaff, tutti, andiamo a cena.

ALL

All in the world's but folly. [40]
Man is born to be jolly,
Spinning and whirling, ever turning,
Living with laughter,
Making a jest
Of all that befalls him,
Passing the test
If he laughs the best
To find the jest
Played on him!

Tutto nel mondo è burla.
L'uom è nato burlone,
La fede in cor gli ciurla,
Gli ciurla la ragione.
Tutti gabbàti! Irride
L'un l'altro ogni mortal.
Ma ride ben chi ride
La risata final.

The curtain falls.

Costume design by Michael Stennett for Falstaff at Covent Garden, 1982. (photo: Donald Southern)

125

Discography Available recordings in stereo (unless asterisked *) and in Italian. Cassette tape numbers are also given. A valuable review of all performances on record is contained in *Opera on Record* (ed. Alan Blyth, Hutchinson 1979).

Conductor Company/Orchestra	*Toscanini* NBC SO	*Solti* RCA Italiana	*Karajan* Philharmonia	*Karajan* Vienna State Opera
Falstaff	Valdengo	Evans	Gobbi	Taddei
Fenton	Madasi	Kraus	Alva	Araiza
Ford	Guarrera	Merrill	Panerai	Panerai
Mrs Ford	Nelli	Ligabue	Schwarzkopf	Kabaivanska
Nannetta	Stich-Randall	Freni	Moffo	Perry
Mrs Page	Merriman	Elias	Merriman	Schmidt
Quickly	Elmo	Simionato	Barbieri	Ludwig
Disc number UK	**AT 301 ***	**2BB104-6**	**SLS 5037**	**6769 060**
Tape number UK		**K110K32**	**TC–SLS 5037**	**7654 060**
Disc number USA	**LM6111 ***	**OSA1395**	**SCL3552**	

Highlights

	Artists	**Number**
Highlights	Corena, Capecchi, Alva Marimpietri, Resnik; New SO, conductor Downes	(UK) SDD 429
L'onore	Evans	SXL 6262
Ford's monologue	Wixell	6580 171
Ehi, Taverniere	Evans, Covent Garden, cond. Downes	SET 392–3
Fairy Song	Ricciarelli, Parma Opera, cond. Patane	SDD 569

Designs by Michael Stennett for 'Falstaff' at Covent Garden, 1982. (photo: Donald Southern)

Bibliography

A detailed study of the composition and score of *Falstaff* concludes the third volume of Julian Budden's three volume *The Operas of Verdi* (Cassell, 1981). It is discussed by Winton Dean in *Shakespeare in Music* (edited by P. Hartnoll, London 1964), and by Vincent Godefroy in the second volume of *The Dramatic Genius of Verdi: Studies of Selected Operas* (London, 1977): a very readable chapter on the opera. A Cambridge University Press Opera Handbook to the opera is in preparation.

Classic biographies remain Francis Toye's *Giuseppe Verdi: His Life and Works* (London, 1931) and Frank Walker's *The Man Verdi* (London, 1962). William Weaver's *Verdi: A Documentary Study* (London, 1977) contains beautiful illustrations and the words of Verdi's contemporaries. Charles Osborne's translation of the Verdi *Letters* is the only one in English.

An English biography of Boito has yet to appear.

The score is published by Ricordi.

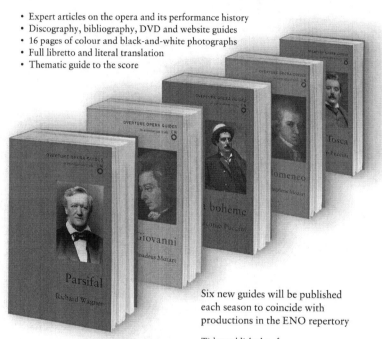